THE
OTHER
MEXICO:
Critique of the Pyramid

THE OTHER MEXICO:

Critique of the Pyramid

by Octavio Paz

translated by Lysander Kemp

GROVE PRESS, INC., NEW YORK

CONTENTS

NOTE

These pages develop and amplify the Hackett Memorial Lecture that I delivered at the University of Texas at Austin on October 30, 1969. Their theme is a reflection upon what has taken place in Mexico since I wrote *The Labyrinth of Solitude*. It is a continuation of that book, but, as I scarcely need to add, it is a critical and self-critical continuation; not only does it extend it and bring it up to date, but it is also a new attempt to decipher reality. Perhaps it would be worth the trouble to explain (once again) that *The Labyrinth of Solitude* was an exercise of the critical imagination: a vision and, simultaneously, a revision—something very different from an essay on Mexican-ness or a search for our supposed being. The Mexican is not an essence but a history. Neither ontology nor psychology. I was and am intrigued not so much by the "national character" as by what that character conceals: by what is behind the mask. From this perspective, the Mexican character performs its function in the same way as that of other peoples and societies: on the one hand, it is a shield, a wall; on the other, a symbol-covered surface, a hieroglyph. As the former, it is a rampart that protects us from the stranger's glance, at the cost of immobilizing and imprisoning us; as the latter, it is a mask that at the same time expresses and suffocates us. Mexican-ness is no more than another example, another variety, of that changing, identical, single, plural creature that each is, all are, none is. Man/ men: perpetual oscillation. The diversity of characters, temperaments, histories, civilizations makes of man, men. And the plural is resolved, is dissolved, in the singular: I, you, he, vanishing as soon as pronounced. Pronouns, like nouns, are masks, and there is no one behind them—except, perhaps, an instantaneous we which is a twinkling of an equally fleeting it. But while we live we can escape neither masks nor nouns and pronouns: we are inseparable from our fictions, our features. We are condemned to invent a mask and to discover afterward that the mask is our true visage. In *The Labyrinth of Solitude* I tried hard (without wholly succeeding, of course) to avoid both the pitfalls of abstract humanism and the illusions of a philosophy of Mexican-ness: the mask that changes into a face, the petrified face that changes into a mask. In those days I was not interested in a definition of Mexican-ness but rather, *as now,* in criticism: that activity which consists not only in knowing ourselves but, just as much or more, in freeing ourselves. Criticism unfolds the possibility of freedom and is thus an invitation to action.

These pages are both a postscript to a book I wrote some twenty years ago and, equally, a preface

to another, unwritten book. I have alluded in two of
my works, *The Labyrinth of Solitude* and *Corriente
alterna* [*Alternating Current*], to that unwritten book:
the theme of Mexico leads to a reflection upon the
fate of Latin America. Mexico is a fragment, a part,
of a vaster history. I do not know whether I am the
most appropriate person to write that book, or, if I
am, whether I will someday be able to do so. On the
other hand, I know that that reflection should be a
recovery of our true history, from the time of Spanish domination and the failure of our revolution of
independence—a failure that corresponds to those of
Spain in the nineteenth and twentieth centuries—to
our own day. I also know that the book should deal
with the problem of development, taking it as its central theme. The contemporary revolutions in Latin
America have been, and are, responses to insufficient
development, and both their historical justification
and their obvious and fatal limitations derive from
this fact. According to the classics of nineteenth-cen-
tury revolutionary thought, revolution would be the
consequence of development: the urban proletariat
would put an end to the inequality between technological and economic development (the way of industrial production) and little or no social progress
(the way of capitalist ownership). The twentieth-
century revolutionary *caudillos* in the underdeveloped or marginal countries have changed revolution
into a way toward development, with the results we
are all familiar with. On the other hand, the models
of development that the West and East offer us today are compendiums of horrors. Can we devise
more humane models that correspond to what we

are? As people on the fringes, inhabitants of the sub-urbs of history, we Latin Americans are uninvited guests who have sneaked in through the West's back door, intruders who have arrived at the feast of mod-ernity as the lights are about to be put out. We arrive late everywhere, we were born when it was already late in history, we have no past or, if we have one, we spit on its remains, our peoples lay down and slept for a century, and while asleep they were robbed and now they go about in rags, we have not been able to save even what the Spaniards left us when they de-parted, we have stabbed one another . . . Despite all this, and despite the fact that our countries are inimical to thought, poets and prose writers and painters who equal the best in the other parts of the world have sprung up here and there, separately but without interruption. Will we now, at last, be capa-ble of thinking for ourselves? Can we plan a society that is not based on the domination of others and that will not end up like the chilling police paradises of the East or with the explosions of disgust and hatred that disrupt the banquet of the West?

The theme of development is intimately linked to that of our identity: who, what, and how we are. I repeat that we are nothing except a relationship: something that can be defined only as a part of a his-tory. The question of Mexico is inseparable from the question of Latin America's future, and this, in turn, is included in another: that of the future relations between Latin America and the United States. The question of ourselves always turns out to be a ques-tion of others. For more than a century that country has appeared to our eyes as a gigantic but scarcely human reality. The United States, smiling or angry, its hand open or clenched, neither sees nor hears us but keeps striding on, and as it does so, enters our lands and crushes us. It is impossible to hold back a giant; it is possible, though far from easy, to make him listen to others; if he listens, that opens the possibility of coexistence. Because of their origins (the Puritan speaks only with God and himself, not with others), and above all because of their power, the North Americans are outstanding in the art of the monologue: they are eloquent and they also know the value of silence. But conversation is not their forte: they do not know how to listen or to reply. Although most of our attempts at a dialogue with them have thus far been unsuccessful, in the last few years we have witnessed certain events that may prefigure a change of attitude. If Latin America is living through a period of revolts and transformations, the United States is also experiencing an upheaval no less violent and profound: the rebellion of Blacks and Chicanos, of women and the young, of artists and intellectuals. The causes that originate and the ideas that inspire these upheavals make them different from those that agitate our own countries, and therefore we would be committing a new error if we attempted to imitate them blindly. But it would not be an error to take note of the capacity for criticism and self-criticism that is unfolding within them—a capacity it would be futile to search for in Latin America. We still have not learned how to think with true freedom. The fault is not intellectual but moral: the worth of a spirit, Nietzsche said, is measured by its capacity for enduring the truth. One of the causes of our incapac-

ity for democratic government is our correlative in-
capacity for critical thinking. The North Americans
—at least the best of them, the conscience of the nation—are trying now to see the truth, their truth,
without shutting their eyes. For the first time in the
history of the United States (earlier, only a few poets
and philosophers voiced it), there is a powerful current of opinion that places under judgment the very
values and beliefs on which Anglo-American civilization has been built. Is that not unprecedented?
This criticism of progress is a portent, a promise of
other changes. If I asked myself, "Can the United
States carry on a dialogue with us?" my answer
would be yes—on condition that first they learn to
speak with themselves, with their own *otherness*:
their Blacks, their Chicanos, their young people. And
something similar must be said to Latin Americans:
criticism of others begins with criticism of oneself.

OCTAVIO PAZ
Austin, 14 December 1969

Translator's Note

This version in English was made from the published text (*Postdata,* Mexico City: Siglo XXI Edi-
tores, 1970) but it incorporates the minor emenda-
tions the author made after that publication and after
reading the translation in typescript.   L.K.

OLYMPICS
AND
TLATELOLCO

1968 was a pivotal year: protests, disturbances, and riots in Prague, Chicago, Paris, Tokyo, Belgrade, Rome, Mexico City, Santiago. Just as the epidemics of the Middle Ages respected neither religious frontiers nor social hierarchies, so the student rebellions annulled ideological classifications. The spontaneous universality of the protest caused a reaction no less spontaneous and universal: the governments invariably attributed the disorders to a conspiracy from without. Although the alleged and secret instigators were almost the same everywhere, their names were shuffled differently in each country. Sometimes there were curious, involuntary coincidences: for example, both the Mexican government and the French Communist party claimed that the students were motivated by agents of Mao and the

CIA. And the absence or, in the case of France, the reticence of the class traditionally considered revolutionary per se—the proletariat—was also notable: up to now, the students' only allies have been the marginal groups which the technological society has not been able, or has not wanted, to integrate. Clearly, we are not facing a recrudescence of the class war but rather a revolt of those sectors to which the technological society has assigned a marginal position, either permanently or temporarily. The students pertain to the second of these categories. In addition, they are the only truly international group: all of the young people of the developed countries pertain to the international subculture of the young, which is produced by a technology that is equally international.

Of all the disaffected sectors, that of the students is the most restless and, with the exception of the North American blacks, the most exasperated. Their exasperation does not spring from particularly hard living conditions but from the paradox that being a student entails: during the long years in which young men and women are isolated in schools of higher education, they live under artificial conditions, half as privileged recluses, half as dangerous irresponsibles. Add to this the extraordinary overcrowding in the universities and the other well-known circumstances that operate as factors of segregation:

real beings in an unreal world. It is true that the alienation of the young is but one of the forms (and among the most benevolent) of the alienation imposed upon everyone by the technological society. It is also true that, because of the very unreality of their situation as inhabitants of a laboratory in which some of the rules of outside society do not apply, the students can reflect on their state and likewise on that of the world around them. The university is at once the object and the condition of student criticism. It is the object of their criticism because it is an institution that segregates the young from the collective life and is thus, in a way, an anticipation of their future alienation. They discover that men are fragmented and separated by modern society: the system, by its very nature, cannot create a true community. And it is the condition of their criticism because, without the distance that the university establishes between the young and the society outside, their criticism would not be possible and the students would immediately enter into the mechanical cycle of production and consumption. The contradiction is irresolvable. If the university were to disappear, so would the possibility of criticism; at the same time, its existence is a proof—and more, a guarantee—of the permanence of the object of criticism, that is, of what it is wished would disappear. The student rebellion oscillates between these two extremes:

its criticism is real, its actions are unreal. The criticism is on target but the actions cannot change society—and in some cases, far from attracting or inspiring other sectors, they even provoke regressions such as that of the French elections of 1968.

Government actions, for their part, have the opacity of all those short-term "realistic" measures that produce, in the long run, cataclysms or decadence. To strengthen the *status quo* is to strengthen a system that grows and spreads at the expense of the people who feed it: as its reality increases, so does our unreality. The technological society distributes ataraxia—that state of equanimous lack of anxiety which the Stoics believed would be achieved by control of the passions—as a panacea for everyone. It does not cure us of the misfortune of being men, but it gratifies us with a stupor that is made up of contented resignation and that does not exclude febrile activity. Yet reality reappears, each time more quickly and more fiercely: crises, violence, explosions. The pivotal year, 1968, showed the universality of the revolt and its ultimate unreality: ataraxia and explosion, but an explosion that dissipates itself, violence that is a new alienation. If the explosions are part of the system, so are the repressions and the lethargy, enforced or voluntary, that follow them. The sickness corroding our societies is constitutional and congenital, not something that comes from without. It is a sickness that has defied all the diagnosticians, both those who call themselves Marxists and those who call themselves heirs of Tocqueville. It is a strange ailment, one that condemns us to incessant development and prosperity—by means of which we multiply our contradictions, inflame our sores, and exacerbate our tendencies toward destruction. And at last the philosophy of progress shows its true face: a featureless blank. We know now that the kingdom of progress is not of this world: the paradise it promises us is in the future, a future that is impalpable, unreachable, perpetual. Progress has peopled history with the marvels and monsters of technology but it has depopulated the life of man. It has given us more things but not more being.

The deeper meaning of the protest movement—not overlooking its reasons and its immediate, circumstantial aims—consists in its having opposed the implacable phantasm of the future with the spontaneous reality of the now. This outbreak of the now signifies the apparition, in the midst of contemporary life, of that forbidden, that damned word "pleasure." A word no less explosive and no less beautiful than the word "justice." When I say "pleasure" I am not thinking of the elaboration of a new hedonism nor of a return to ancient sensual wisdom—although the former would not be calamitous and the latter would be desirous—but rather of the revelation of that dark half of man that has been humiliated and buried by the morality of progress: the half that reveals itself in the images of art and love. The definition of man as a being that works should be changed to that of a being that desires. This is the tradition which extends from Blake to the surrealist poets and which the young have taken up: the prophetic tradition of Western poetry since the German Romantic movement. For the first time since the philosophy of progress grew from the ruins of the medieval universe, the young are questioning the validity and meaning of the very principles that underlie the modern age—and they are doing so within the most advanced and progressive society in the world, the United States. This questioning reflects neither hatred for reason and science, nor nostalgia for the Neolithic age (although Lévi-Strauss and other anthropologists tell us that the Neolithic was probably the only happy age that man has known). On the contrary, the question they ask is one that only a technological society can ask itself, and the answer to it will determine the fate of the world we have made. Past, present, or future—which is the true time of man, in which is his kingdom? And if his kingdom is in the present, how can the now, by nature explosive and orgiastic, be inserted in historical time? Modern society must answer these questions about the now—*right now*. The other alternative is to perish in a suicidal explosion or to sink deeper and deeper into the current process in which the production of goods is in danger of becoming less than the production of refuse.

The universality of youthful protest has not prevented it from assuming specific characteristics in each region of the world. As I have said, the youth movement in the United States and Europe poses implicit, unformulated questions about the very foundations of the modern age and that which has been, since the eighteenth century, its guiding principle. These questions arise in the countries of Eastern Europe in a very diluted form, and in Latin America they never rise at all except as empty slogans. The reason for this is clear: the North Americans and Europeans are the only ones who have a really complete experience of what progress is and of what it means. In the West the young rebel against the mechanisms of the technological society, against its tantalizing world of objects that wear out and vanish almost as soon as we possess them (as if they were an involuntary and conclusive confirmation of the illusory character that the Buddhists attribute to reality), against the overt or covert violence which that society brings to bear upon its minorities or, in foreign affairs, upon other peoples. In the countries of Eastern Europe, on the other hand, the struggle of the young presents two features that are absent in the West: nationalism and democracy. Nationalism in opposition to Soviet domination of and interference in those countries, and democracy in opposition to the Communist bureaucracies governing political and economic life. It is significant that the latter seems the immediate and primordial means of recovery to the youth of the East: in the West, the word "democracy" has lost almost all of its magnetism. This symptom is terrifying: whatever may be the limitations of Western democracy (which are many and grave: bureaucratic rule by parties, monopolies of information, corruption, et cetera), there can be no political life without freedom of criticism and a variety of opinions and groups. For us, as modern men, political life is synonymous with rational, civilized life. This is true even for nations that have inherited a high civilization and that, like ancient China, never knew democracy. The young fanatics who recite the catechism of Mao—by the way, a mediocre academic poet—commit not only an aesthetic and intellectual error but also a moral one. Critical thinking cannot be sacrificed on the altars of accelerated economic development, the revolutionary idea, the leader's prestige and infallibility, or any other mirage of that sort. The experiences of Russia and Mexico are conclusive: without democracy, economic development has no meaning, even though that development has

been gigantic in the former and far more modest
—though proportionally no less remarkable—in
the latter. Every dictatorship, whether of man
or of party, leads to the two forms that schizo-
phrenia loves most: the monologue and the
mausoleum. Moscow and Mexico City are full
of gagged people and monuments to the Revolution.

The student movement in Mexico was in
some ways like those in other countries, both of the
West and of Eastern Europe. It seems to me that
the closest affinities were with those in the latter
countries: nationalism, reacting not against Soviet intervention but against North American imperialism; aspirations for democratic reform; and
protest, not against Communist bureaucracies but
against the Institutional Revolutionary Party.
But this revolt of Mexican youth was singular,
as is the country itself. There is not any dubious
nationalism in this statement. Mexico is a country
that occupies an eccentric position in Western
civilization—it is "Castilian streaked with Aztec,"
as the Mexican poet López Velarde wrote—and
within Latin America its historical situation is
also unique: Mexico lives in a post-revolutionary
period while the majority of the other Latin
American countries are going through a pre-
revolutionary stage. Finally, its economic development has been exceptional. After a prolonged

and bloody period of violence, the Mexican Revolution was able to create original institutions and a new state. For the last forty years, and especially for the last two decades, the nation's economy has made such strides that economists and sociologists point to Mexico as an example for other underdeveloped countries. The statistics are indeed impressive, especially if one keeps in mind the condition of the nation when the Revolution broke out in 1910, as well as the material and human destruction it suffered during more than ten years of civil strife. In order to gain international recognition of its transformation into a modern or semi-modern country, Mexico requested, and was granted, the designation of its capital as the site of the 1968 Olympic Games. The organizers of the Games not only passed the test successfully, they even added an original program to that of the sports events, a program underlining the pacific, noncompetitive nature of the Mexican Olympics: exhibits of international art; concerts, plays, and dance presentations by orchestras and companies from all over the world; an international meeting of poets; and other events of a similar nature. But, in the context of the student revolt and the repression that ensued, these celebrations seemed nothing but gaudy gestures designed to hide the realities of a country stirred and terrified by governmental violence. Thus, at the very moment in which the Mexican government was receiving international recognition for forty years of political stability and economic progress, a swash of blood dispelled the official optimism and caused every citizen to doubt the meaning of that progress.

The student movement began as a street brawl between rival groups of adolescents. Police brutality united them. Later, as the repression became more severe and the hostility of the press, radio, and television—almost all pro-government —increased, the movement strengthened, expanded, and grew aware of itself. In the course of a few weeks it became clear that the young students, without having expressly intended it, were the spokesmen of the people. Let me emphasize that they were not the spokesmen of this or that class but of the collective conscience. From the very beginning an attempt was made to isolate the movement by placing it in quarantine, in order to prevent the spread of ideological infection. The leaders and officials of the labor unions hastened to condemn the students in menacing terms; so did the official political parties of the left and of the right, though with less vehemence. Despite the mobilization of all the means of propaganda and moral coercion, not to mention the physical violence of the police and the army, the people spontaneously joined the student demonstrations, and one of them, the famous "Silent Demonstration," brought together about 400,000 people, something never before seen in Mexico.

Unlike the French students in May of the same year, the Mexican students did not propose violent and revolutionary social changes, nor was their program as radical as those of many groups of German and North American youths. It also lacked the orgiastic and near-religious tone of the "hippies." The movement was democratic and reformist, even though some of its leaders were of the extreme left. Was this a tactical maneuver? I think it would be more sensible to attribute that moderation to the circumstances themselves and to the weight of objective reality: the temper of the Mexican people is not revolutionary and neither are the historical conditions of the country. Nobody wants a revolution. What the people do want is reform: an end to the rule of privilege initiated by the National Revolutionary Party forty years ago. The students' demands were genuinely moderate: derogation of one article in the Penal Code, an article that is completely unconstitutional and that contains the affront to human rights called "crime of opinion"; the freeing of various political prisoners; the dismissal of the chief of police; et cetera. All of their petitions could be summed up in a single word that was both the crux of the movement and the key to its magnetic influence on the conscience of the people: *democratization*. Again and again the demonstrators asked for "a public dialogue between the government and the students" as a prelude to a dialogue between the people and the authorities. This demand was an echo of that which a group of us writers had made in 1958, during similar but less widespread disturbances that foretold much worse ones to come—as we warned the government at the time.

The attitude of the students gave the government an opportunity to correct its policies without losing face. It would have been enough to listen to what the people were saying through their student spokesmen. They were not expecting a radical change, but they did expect greater flexibility and a return to the tradition of the Mexican Revolution, a tradition that was never dogmatic and that was very sensitive to changes in popular feeling. In this way the government could have broken out of the prison of words and concepts in which it had enclosed and isolated itself, the prison of all those formulas that nobody believes in any longer and that are summed up in the grotesque expression with which the official family describes the only political party: the Institutional Revolution. By freeing itself from its prison of words, the government could also have broken out of another prison—a realer one—that surrounded and paralyzed it: the prison of business and of the interests of bankers and financiers. A return to com-

municating with the people would have meant a
recovery of the authority and freedom to carry
on a dialogue with the right, the left, and the
United States. With great clarity and concision,
Daniel Cosío Villegas, one of the keenest and
most honest minds in Mexico, pointed out what,
in his opinion (and, I should add, in the opinion
of most thinking Mexicans), was "the only remedy: to make public life truly public." The government preferred to resort, alternately, to physical force and institutional-revolutionary rhetoric.
This oscillation probably reflected a struggle between the technocrats, desirous of saving what
little was left of the revolutionary tradition, and
the political bureaucracy, which favored a strong
hand. But at no time did the government show
any desire to "make public life truly public," and
to begin a dialogue with the people. The authorities did propose negotiations, but behind the
scenes, and the talks aborted because the students
refused to accept this immoral procedure.

Near the end of September the army occupied the University and the Polytechnical Institute. This action was so widely criticized that the
troops withdrew from both institutions. There
was a breathing spell. The students, full of hope,
gathered for a meeting—not a demonstration—
in the Plaza of Tlatelolco on the second of October. At the end of the meeting, when those
attending it were about to leave, the plaza was

surrounded by the army and the killing began. A few hours later it was all over. How many died? No newspaper in Mexico dared to print the number of deaths. Here is the figure that the English newspaper *The Guardian,* after a careful investigation, considered the most probable: 325. Thousands must have been injured, thousands must have been arrested. The second of October, 1968, put an end to the student movement. It also ended an epoch in the history of Mexico.

Although student uprisings are a world-wide phenomenon, they break out with the greatest virulence in the most advanced societies. It could be said, therefore, that the student movement and the Olympic Games in Mexico were complementary events: both of them were signs that the country was relatively developed. What was discordant, and anomalous, and unforeseen, was the attitude of the government. How can it be explained? On the one hand, the students' petitions did not endanger the regime, and it was not faced with a revolutionary situation. On the other hand, no action by any government—not even that of France, which was menaced by a revolutionary tide—had the ferocity, there is no other word for it, of the repression in Mexico. The world press, in spite of the daily ration of horrors it dispenses, was shocked. A popular North American magazine, rather appalled but in a maidenly way, said that what happened in Mexico was a typical case of "overreaction," a symptom of "the sclerosis of the Mexican regime." A curious understatement. In any living organism, an exaggerated or excessive reaction indicates fear and insecurity, and sclerosis is a sign not only of old age but also of an inability to change. The regime showed that it was neither willing nor able to examine its own conscience; but without criticism, above all without self-criticism, there is no possibility of change.

This mental and moral weakness led to the physical violence. Like those neurotics who retreat when confronted with new and difficult situations, who swing from fear to rage, who commit insensate acts in a regression to the instinctive behavior of infants or animals, the government regressed to earlier periods in the history of Mexico. Aggression is synonymous with regression. It was an instinctive repetition that took the form of an expiatory ritual. Its resemblances to Mexico's past, especially to the Aztec world, are fascinating, frightening, and repellent. The massacre at Tlatelolco shows us that the past which we thought was buried is still alive and has burst out among us. Each time it appears in public it is both masked and armed, and we cannot tell what it is, except that it is vengeance and destruction. It is a past that we have not been able to recognize, to name, to unmask. But before discussing this theme—which is the central and secret theme of our history—I must describe in its broad outlines the development of modern Mexico, that paradoxical development in which the simultaneous existence of contradictory elements is symbolized by those two words, "Olympics" and "Tlatelolco."

DEVELOPMENT
AND
OTHER
MIRAGES

Mexico, 1920: the military overthrow of the old regime had hardly been accomplished when the country had to face the danger that threatens every victorious revolution—anarchy. The quarrels among the different factions that made up the revolutionary movement were no less violent than the armed rebellion of the people against the autocracy of Porfirio Díaz and his professional army. Those factions were more personalistic than ideological, but in a rudimentary form they already represented the interests and tendencies of the country's different classes and groups: peasants, farmers, the petite bourgeoisie, the growing working class, et cetera. Although the recently adopted Constitution of 1917 foresaw a peaceful transference of power by means of democratic elections, the reality was very different: there were no political parties and the country was ruled by the revolutionary dictatorship, that is, by the dictatorship of the military chieftains of the Revolution. The struggle among factions was never democratic; political supremacy was achieved, not by the number of votes, but by the number of soldiers and guns. Each presidential election degenerated into an armed struggle that ended with the death of one or various of the aspirants to power and of many of their followers, not to mention the innocent people dragged into the conflict. After the fall of Porfirio Díaz, it seemed as if the country was condemned to repeat again—and forever—the monotonous, bloody cycle of dictatorship followed by anarchy, anarchy followed by dictatorship. But the progressive and violent elimination of military chieftains led to a regime which, if not democratic, was also not self-destructive. The first measure—a negative one—was the constitutional prohibition of presidential re-election. This ruled out personal dictatorship. The second measure—a positive one—was the founding, in 1929, of the National Revolutionary Party. That established the revolutionary dictatorship—or, to be more exact, the dictatorship of the group that won in the struggle among factions.

The National Revolutionary Party was an association of military and political leaders gathered around General Plutarco Elías Calles. As an agent and civil branch of revolutionary power, the party had no strength by itself; its power was a reflection of the power of the *caudillo* and of the bosses and military men who ruled in the provinces. Nevertheless, as peace spread and as the country began to return to normal, the party gained strength—not at the expense of the *caudillo* but of the generals. The dual political structure of contemporary Mexico was already there in embryo: the president and the party. The function of the new organism was above all negative: not so much to set up a program as to reduce the clashes among factions and to put down troublemakers. Although it was not a seed of democracy, it was the beginning of a national political structure, tightly bound to the new state. The most significant of the words that formed its name was the first: the National Revolutionary Party fought against and debilitated the power of the regional bosses.

In 1938, President Lázaro Cárdenas changed not only the party's name but also its composition and its program. The social base of the Party of the Mexican Revolution was wider than that of the National Revolutionary Party and it brought together four groups: the workers, the peasants, the popular sector, and the military. It was an attempt to create a functional democracy rather than a political democracy. The party became an efficient instrument: it was the eyes and ears of a fine and generous president, Lázaro Cárdenas. Although its slogan was "For a democracy of workers," the Party of the Mexican Revolution was not democratic either. If no one remembers its debates, that is because there were none; its policies never were the product of public deliberation but rather of what was dictated by President Cárdenas. Even the inclusion in the party of the worker and peasant groups, far from strengthening them, contributed to their eventual servitude. According to most historians, the Revolution as such ended in the decade between 1940 and 1950. Since then, economic development and industrialization have become the immediate and primordial objectives of the regime. This policy was initiated by Miguel Alemán, a president no less energetic than Cárdenas. In 1946, Alemán changed the name of the party once again, to that by which it is now known, a name that courageously illustrates the paradoxes of politics rather than those of logic: the Institutional Revolutionary Party.

The three names of the party reflect the three stages of modern Mexico: creation of a new state, social reform, and economic development. But none of the tendencies that characterize these three stages arose from the party; they came down from above, from the president and his advisors. The party has produced not a single idea, not a single program, in its forty years of existence! It is not a political organization in the proper sense of the term; its recruiting methods are not democratic, and it develops neither programs nor strategies for realizing them. It is a bureaucratic organism that performs political-administrative functions. Its principal mission is political domination, not by physical force but by the control and manipulation of the people through the bureaucracies that direct the labor unions and the associations of the peasants and the middle class. In this task it has the support of the government and the benevolent neutrality or outright partisanship of almost all of the information media: political monopoly entails control not only of popular organizations but also of public opinion. At the same time, the party is an organ for exploring the conscience of the people and their tendencies and aspirations. This is a prime function, one which, in the past, gave the party flexibility, vitality, even popularity, but which now, because of its hierarchical organization and the sclerosis that for some years has paralyzed it more and more, it performs with increasing inefficiency. The party's deafness increases in direct proportion to the increase in popular dissent.

In its ways of functioning and its immoderate use of revolutionary jargon, the party could be thought to resemble the Communist parties of Eastern Europe: both it and they are political bureaucracies affixed to the national economy, although the economies of those countries are state economies and ours is mixed. But the party is not an ideological party, it is one of groups and interests—a circumstance which, if it has favored venality, has also saved us from the terrors of any sort of orthodoxy. The variety of tendencies that exist within it—I should say, that until recently existed within it—could make it resemble the Congress Party of India, except for this important difference: the Mexican party has no internal democracy and is dominated by a group of hierarchs who, for their part, give blind obedience to each president in turn. This has been especially unfortunate because the diversity of currents and opinions within the party—a reflection of those that divide the nation and make up its political and social reality—would have allowed it to attempt an experiment which, besides vitalizing and regenerating the regime, would have offered a solution to the crisis in which the country has been living for more than ten years: initiating democratic reform within the party itself. But perhaps now it is too late: the massacre of October 2 wiped out that possibility with blood.

By safeguarding the continuity of the government, the party has been a force for peace and stability. The revolutionary leaders, confronted with the nightmare of personal dictatorship limited only by the power of the *caudillo* and ending almost always in a bloody explosion, conceived an institutional dictatorship that was both limited and impersonal. The president has immense power but can occupy the post for only a single term; the power he wields comes to him from his investiture and disappears when he leaves office. The principles of rotation and selection operate within the party: to be president, or governor, or senator, or deputy, one must work through the party ranks, carry out one's assignments, move upward step by step. For political and governmental leaders the Institutional Revolutionary Party is a school, a laboratory, and a sieve. Promotions are achieved as in any other bureaucracy: the requirements are discipline, *esprit de corps,* respect for the hierarchies, seniority, administrative capacity, dedication, efficiency, quickness, smoothness, and desperate energy. One is promoted by consent of one's superiors. Although the party is contemptuous of democratic elections, it does respect the aristocratic veto power: the president has the unquestioned right to choose his successor, though first he must consult the former presidents and the high functionaries. The unwritten law is that his candidate will at least not provoke the opposition of these leaders. Each of them represents powerful interests, from those of private enterprise to those of the bureaucracies of the labor unions and the peasant organizations. The veto power pertains especially to former presidents. They are the voice of tradition and represent revolutionary continuity. They are something akin to a council of the elders.

Veto power, then—but not the power to criticize. The Institutional Revolutionary Party has never been critical of presidential actions; on the contrary, it has given them its unconditional support. In Mexico there is a horror—it would not be too much to call it a sacred horror—of anything like intellectual criticism and dissidence. A difference of opinion instantly and unconsciously becomes a personal quarrel. This is particularly true with regard to the president: criticism of his policies becomes a sacrilege. I should add that this veneration disappears when he steps down. His civic attributes are venerated, but not his person. Those attributes cover him up like the masks that hid the faces of the ancient Mexican deities, and they transform him, literally, into an image. Fanatical respect for the person of the *caudillo* is of Arabic origin and can be found throughout the Hispanic world; among the Mexicans, the religious reverence inspired by the impersonal attributes of the president has its roots in the Aztec world. I will return to this point later; for the moment I will only remark that the Senate and the Chamber of Deputies have been, and still are, two groups of chatterers and flatterers who never offer any criticism whatsoever; that the judicial power is mute and impotent; that freedom of the press is more a formality than a reality; and that radio and television are in the hands of two or three families who are more interested in earning money by brutalizing the audience than in analyzing the country's problems honestly and objectively. Furthermore, as proprietor of the party and the information media, the president enjoys an almost unlimited authority to use federal funds. It is really extraordinary that with such powers in their hands our presidents have not been Caligulas and Neros. Perhaps the reason lies in the long years of self-control which the party imposes on the faithful. Once again we see the organic relationship between the presidency and the party. From the very beginning they have been complementary realities; they were a response to a crisis situation, and represented a compromise between the personal dictatorship of the *caudillos* and the democratic program of the Mexican Revolution.

The virtues and defects of the Institutional Revolutionary Party are obvious. Among the former, the most important is its gradually achieved independence from the military. The party stands for the principle of separation between the nation's military and its political leaders, something that most Latin American countries have not yet accomplished. Can it preserve that independence in the future? I doubt it very much. Most of the writers concerned with modern Mexican history believe that the party has outlived itself, but they point out that, whatever its defects, it made a powerful contribution to the country's peace and stability, without which economic development would have been impossible. Although I agree with this opinion, I ask myself whether many of the defects in our development are not the direct fault of the party. If it is true that it preserved the continuity of governmental action, it is likewise true that it stifled both analysis and criticism of that action. Furthermore, and above all, it protected the irresponsible and venal bureaucrats in charge of carrying out the programs of economic development. And there is something else: although the party was conceived as a desperate remedy for a seemingly chronic illness that threatened to destroy the country—that is, the danger of continuing the cycle of dictatorship, anarchy, dictatorship—it now perpetuates a regime of transitions and exceptions. The only dictatorship in Mexico is that of the Institutional Revolutionary Party, and the only danger of anarchy is that which is provoked by the unnatural prolongation of its political monopoly.

It was during the Second World War that the actual revolutionary period of modern Mexico came to an end and the period of economic development began. The process has been similar, though not identical, in every country in which revolutionary movements have triumphed without first having an economic base capable of financing social reforms. This is the great limitation—it would be more exact to say condemnation—of every revolution in the underdeveloped countries, not excluding, of course, either Russia or China. There is an inescapable contradiction between development and social reform, a contradiction that is always resolved in favor of the former. In Mexico's case the change in orientation was due mainly to these three circumstances: the regime's decision to go ahead with industrialization, if only on a small scale, as the only cure for the country's ailments; the influence of the United States; and the appearance of a new capitalist class. The first of these was the determining factor. During the course of the war, Mexico discovered that although the prices for its raw materials had risen considerably on the international market, it could not purchase anything in that market; a little later, in the postwar period, it discovered that a downward fluctuation in the prices for those materials, along with a rise in the prices for manufactured products, not only devoured all of its savings but also impeded capitalization and, therefore, development. In order to counteract, insofar as possible, the disadvantageous conditions imposed by the international market, the government set about to diversify production so as to make our economy less vulnerable and dependent. Thanks to our resources—and our efforts—we have been more fortunate in this than other countries. Cuba, for example, still depends on sugar. Our rapid development in the last twenty years would not have been possible without that diversification of production and the bonanza of 1940–1950—without those economic circumstances and, I should add, without the government's determination to change the country's economic structure: the political decision was no less important than the economic opportunity.

The influence of the United States was considerable but not central. Its economic presence was no less powerful in other countries, yet they have not undergone the structural changes that Mexico has. Since this topic has provoked and still provokes many arguments, I should analyze it briefly. The only way that weak countries can defend themselves against the strong ones is to take maximum advantage of the quarrels among the great powers. This has been the policy of Mexico's governments. The rules of the game are simple: the greater the number of world powers, the greater the freedom of movement for small and middle-sized countries. But the game has become more difficult since World War II. First, all the intermediate positions were wiped out by an alliance between the North Americans and the Russians; immediately afterward, the alliance was replaced by a rivalry that polarized nations into two irreconcilable groups. The absence of an independent international policy in the countries of Western Europe (the alternative of Gaullism arrived too late for Mexico), the expansionist and nationalistic character of Stalinist Russia, and the aggressive and intransigent attitude of John Foster Dulles accentuated the defensive nature of Mexico's international politics. And it should not be forgotten that since 1840 Mexico's policy toward the United States has been and is essentially defensive. In spite of difficulties and contradictions, the government maintained our tradition on the international front, though each time with greater timidity, greater formality: the change that took place was internal. Although external pressures favored that change, considerations of an internal nature were decisive. The government had either to accommodate itself to industrialization or resign itself to stagnation, and it chose the former alternative. This decision led it to another, that of making the private sector an essential part of the development program and, therefore, of favoring it as much as possible. Since Mexican capitalism was in its infancy, it was decided—not without much hesitation and internal dispute—that the international private sector (North American) should also participate in the task of economic development. As a result, Mexico's economic dependence was accentuated.

Here I must insert a digression, not on economics—I am no expert in such matters—but on historical evidence. The reality of the United States' economic and political imperialism is a fact that needs no demonstrating: it has been analyzed again and again. But the opposition between the United States and Latin America is not only of an economic and political nature: the dichotomy is both older and more profound. Imperialism could vanish tomorrow, either because of a change of regime in the United States or, more likely, because science and technology will have discovered substitutes for our raw materials and because the economies of the most advanced countries will have become progressively more self-sufficient. In the near future, perhaps, the developed countries will not even bother to fleece the underdeveloped: they will leave them to their poverty and their convulsions. But this does not mean that we will cease to be what we are now, the scene of their disputes and the field of their battles. What I want to emphasize is that the disappearance of economic imperialism would not imply a leveling of power:

as long as this inequality of forces exists, so will the United States' domination over the rest of the hemisphere. The inequality is the same among capitalist countries as among those that call themselves socialist. Witnesses: Santo Domingo and Prague. Let us suppose that even this inequality disappears: the opposition would persist because it lives in strata more profound than economic and political organization. I am speaking of realities that the modern world has stubbornly forgotten or denied but that now reappear with still greater force: the whole complex of attitudes toward the world and the otherworld, life and death, the I and the other, that make up what we call a civilization.

Although the Russians, Chinese, and Japanese have embraced the cause of modernity and progress—two Western ideas—with the same frenzy, they are still, and will continue to be, Russians, Chinese, Japanese: they will be different and the same, like the gryphon Dante saw in Purgatory. Duzèmil has shown that the tripartite structure of Indo-European ideology has endured for millenniums, despite the fact that those societies experienced changes even more profound than those which modern nations have suffered. The change from a nomadic society to great urban civilizations during the second millennium before Christ was no less radical than the leap from feudalism to the modern age; nonetheless, the ideological substratum, as Duzèmil calls it, persisted and persists. The example of psychoanalysis saves me from wasting time on a boring proof: the persistence of infantile traumas and psychic structures in the life of an adult is equivalent to the permanence of certain historical—or better, intrahistorical—structures in societies. Those structures are the origin of the bundles of distinctive traits that are civilizations. Civilizations: styles of living and dying.

True, the opposition between the United States and Latin America is not an opposition between civilizations: it pertains instead to the subgenus of contradictions within the same civilization. But, having admitted this, I want to point out that the differences are fundamental, as I tried to demonstrate at some length in *The Labyrinth of Solitude*. This opposition could be fecund, of course, if the arrogance of one party and the anxiety of the other did not muffle and vitiate the dialogue. But even under the best of conditions these dialogues are difficult: as soon as a conversation between North Americans and Latin Americans moves beyond informative and quantitative matters, it becomes a hazardous walking-in-circles among quibbles, ambiguities, and errors. The truth is that they are not dialogues at all, they are monologues: neither of us ever hears what the other is saying—or, if we do hear, we always think the other was saying something else. Even poetry and other literary forms do not escape from this tangle of confusions. The majority of North American poets and writers ignore or look down on the culture and/or people of Latin America. An example of the former: in the *Cantos* of Ezra Pound, that great monument to the encyclopedic voracity of the United States, all civilizations and all peoples make a showing except the pre-Columbian world and Spanish-Portuguese America: no Mayan temples or baroque churches, no *Popul Vuh* or Sor Juana de la Cruz. An example of the latter: almost all of the North Americans who have written about Latin America, not excepting so distinguished a poet as Wallace Stevens, have invariably been exalted by our indigenous past or by our landscapes but, just as invariably, have considered the contemporary Latin American to be insignificant. Latin America: ruins and scenery, with here and there a dim, bungling human being—the waiter and manager at the hotel. As for the Latin American vision of the United States, it is colossal and chimerical: to Rubén Darío, the first Roosevelt was none other than a reincarnation of Nebuchadnezzar; when Jorge Luis Borges visited Texas, the first thing that occurred to him was to write a poem in honor of the defenders of the Alamo. Exaggerated wrath, or envy, or obsequiousness: we think of the United States, simultaneously and without contradiction, as Goliath, Polyphemus, and Pantagruel.

In his lucid essay, "The Mexican Revolution, Then and Now," the historian Daniel Cosío Villegas asserts that the Mexican government has become a prisoner of the new capitalist class and is thus paying for its initial mistake, which was that of giving the private sector a central role in the program of industrialization and development.* This assertion, though basically correct, should be slightly modified. I will begin by underlining a fact that has been little commented on: that the new class is a deliberate creation of the revolutionary regime, much as the capitalist class in Japan was created by the movement toward modernization following the Meiji restoration. In both cases, the relationship that Marxism had made familiar to us—and whose real nature it had oversimplified—was turned upside down: the state is less an expression of the dominant class, at least in origin, than the dominant class is a result of the actions of the state. Another factor to take into consideration is the existence of the Institutional Revolutionary Party as a relatively autonomous bureaucratic-political organization that includes bureaucracies of the worker and peasant organizations. This characteristic is not found in other countries,

---

* Daniel Cosío Villegas, *Change in Latin America* (Lincoln: University of Nebraska Press, 1960).

except those that call themselves socialist. The Institutional Revolutionary Party is bound up with Mexican capitalism but it is not Mexican capitalism itself. In analyzing the new class of entrepreneurs, Frank R. Brandenburg said that the "Alemán regime originated a dual class; some of its members headed private companies and the others took over the direction of government enterprises." * Among the latter there is that large group of technocrats who have taken it upon themselves to defend, with varying success, the legacy of the Mexican Revolution. This sector is distinct from that of the party, and it constitutes the other bureaucracy of the new state, a bureaucracy of technicians and administrators, as the party is a bureaucracy of politicians. Brandenburg remarks that the new class of private entrepreneurs "rarely occupies official positions, although many politicians move on from managing public affairs to managing private businesses." Hence, not only is there a margin of independence between the private sector and the public, but also the party maintains considerable autonomy. The official left wing, the technocrats within the government, and many groups of intellectuals, have always speculated on the possibility that the government, taking courage from the strength of the party and of the popular sectors it controls,

---

* Frank R. Brandenburg, *The Making of Modern Mexico* (Englewood Cliffs: Prentice-Hall, 1964).

will some day stand up to private enterprise and to imperialism. It seems to me that the second of October dissipated those hopes. To stand up to the bankers and financiers, the party would first have to recover its influence over the popular classes, and to do that it would have to transform and democratize itself, something it cannot and does not wish to do. Furthermore, since the party is beginning to show an alarming inability to control the waves of discontent and protest, the private sector will sooner or later be tempted to free itself from the party. Here again are the alternatives arising from the student movement, the alternatives that conclude any analysis of the present situation in Mexico: democratization or political immobility and, afterwards, violence.

The economic development of Mexico would have been impossible without the three circumstances—industrialization, the influence of the United States, and the new capitalist class—which I have just described. There is still another one, equally important: the revolutionary reforms, though they failed to create a new social order, did break up the great landholdings of the old regime, thus freeing the social forces that have changed the face of Mexico in the last twenty years. I will mention only the most outstanding changes: the rate of economic growth has been constantly higher than the rate of demographic growth, even though the latter is one of the highest in the world; real per capita income has also increased throughout this period; the construction of a communications network has ended the traditional isolation of the towns and villages; a relatively solid economic infrastructure has been created; the country has completed the first stage of industrialization—that is, it needs to import fewer and fewer consumer goods—and is now preparing, with some difficulty, for the second stage; important advances have been made in agriculture—thanks to agrarian reform, irrigation, the creation of new types of seeds, and other factors, Mexico is now able to feed itself; and important progress has been made in public health and public education, although the latter is still sadly inadequate, especially in the area of secondary and higher education. All of these facts can be summed up in the following: the emergence of a working class, a middle class, and a capitalist class. It would seem as if the old dream of the Mexican liberals of the nineteenth century has been realized: Mexico at last is a modern country. The trouble is that if you look at the picture carefully enough, you can see vast areas of shadow. It is a disturbing sort of modernity.

Mexico's economic development did not follow a long-range national plan. Some regions have been favored with the government's solicitude and credits, while others have been almost completely neglected. This appalling horizontal inequality is matched by another that is vertical: although the index of poverty has continuously gone down during the last thirty years, the decrease has been far from proportional to economic growth. In absolute numbers there are more rich people today than there were thirty years ago, but also many more poor people, though the proportion of the latter has diminished. Hence the country's economic development has been notable but its social development most certainly has not. Mexico continues to be a country of scandalous inequalities. In the light of this, it is not difficult to infer the principal defect in our industrialization, a defect which the North American economist Sanford Mosk pointed out almost twenty years ago: the weakness of our internal market. If the government does not attack this problem by enlarging the present market and strengthening the people's buying power, the rhythm of development will slow down and even halt. To launch this attack, it must implement a policy of social reform and it must re-establish freedom within the labor unions, which at present are controlled by an affluent bureaucracy. Without a policy of social integration and without real freedom of negotiation for the workers, Mexico's development will be interrupted. The relationship has been turned around. At first it was imperative to achieve economic progress; but now, for this progress to continue, it is equally imperative to achieve social development—that is, justice.

In a recent book, James W. Wilkie sums up the three stages of evolution of modern Mexico in this way: "Political revolution destroyed the old institutional order; it did not create a democratic state. Social revolution attacked the old structure of society; it did not bring about a new one, either economically or socially. Economic revolution brought industrialization to a high point; it did not create balanced economic growth or a large internal market." * These conclusions are essentially correct, but they overlook one fundamental characteristic of the contemporary situation: the existence of two Mexicos, one modern and the other underdeveloped. This duality is the result of the Revolution and of the development that followed it: thus, it is the source of many hopes and, at the same time, of future threats. Here is the dilemma: either the developed Mexico will absorb and integrate the other, or the underdeveloped Mexico, by the sheer dead weight of demographic increase, will end up by strangling the developed Mexico. Until now, the first Mexico has grown and the second has di-

---

* James W. Wilkie, *The Mexican Revolution: Federal Expenditure and Social Changes Since 1910* (Berkeley: University of California Press, 1967).

minished, though not with the speed and in the proportions that are desirable and, above all, possible. According to Pablo González Casanova, the positive element in the present situation is social mobility: "The peasants of yesterday are the workers of today and the sons of those workers can be the professionals of tomorrow." But the same sociologist warns that it is urgently necessary to reorient the country's economic development, which should fulfill a social and national function, for otherwise the distance between the two Mexicos will continue to increase. I believe we all agree in thinking that any attempt at reform or transformation must be preceded by a democratic reform of the regime. Only in an atmosphere of freedom and openness to criticism can the true problems of Mexico be defined and discussed. Some of them are immense—for instance, the population explosion—but the government has not even attempted to discuss them.

When we consider what is happening both in our country and in other parts of the world, we are forced to take another look at the idea of development at top speed and at any cost. Let us forget for a moment the crimes and stupidities that have been committed in the name of development from Communist Russia to India, from the Argentina of Perón to the Egypt of Nasser, and let us look at what is happening in the United States and Western Europe: the destruction of the ecological balance, the contamination of lungs and of spirits, the psychic damage to the young, the abandoning of the elderly, the erosion of the sensibilities, the corruption of the imagination, the debasement of sex, the accumulation of wastes, the explosions of hatred. Faced as we are by all this, how can we not turn away and seek another mode of development? It is an urgent task that requires both science and imagination, both honesty and sensitivity; a task without precedence, because all of the modes of development that we know, whether they come from the West or the East, lead to disaster. Under the present circumstances the race toward development is mere haste to reach ruin. But we are forbidden to speak of these themes while we still have not achieved the minimal requirement: that free atmosphere that is the natural space in which both critical thought and the imagination unfold.

Political crises are moral crises. In 1943, in a well-known article, Jesús Silva Herzog declared that the Revolution was suffering a crisis, perhaps a mortal crisis, and that the illness was more moral than physical. Those years saw the beginnings of the third period of our contemporary history, a stage that the North American historian Stanley R. Ross has called the Mexican Thermidor: ideas were transformed into formulas and the formulas into masks. Although moralists are scandalized by the fortunes amassed by the old revolutionaries, they have failed to observe that this material flowering has a verbal parallel: oratory has become the favorite literary genre of the prosperous. More than a style, it is a stamp, a class distinction. And alongside oratory, with its plastic flowers, there is the barbarous syntax of our newspapers, the foolishness of North American television programs with the Spanish dubbed in by persons who know neither English nor Spanish, the daily dishonoring of the language on loudspeakers and the radio, the loathsome vulgarities of advertising—all that asphyxiating rhetoric, that sugary, nauseating rhetoric, of satisfied people whose gluttony has made them lethargic. Seated at Mexico, the new lords and their courtesans and parasites lick their lips over a gigantic platter of choice garbage. When a society decays, it is language that is first to become gangrenous. As a result, social criticism begins with grammar and the re-establishing of meanings. This is what has happened in Mexico. Criticism of the present state of affairs was begun, not by the moralists, not by the radical revolutionaries, but by the writers (a handful of the older but a majority of the younger). Their criticism has not been directly political—though they have not shied away from treating political themes in their works—but instead verbal: the exercise of criticism as an exploration of language and the exercise of language as an exploration of reality.

The new literature, poetry as well as the novel, began by being at once a reflection on language and an attempt at creating a new language: a system of transparencies, to provoke reality into making an appearance. But to realize this proposal it was indispensable to cleanse the language, to flush away the official rhetoric. Hence these writers had to deal with two tendencies inherited from the Revolution and now thoroughly corrupt: nationalism and an "art of the people." Both tendencies had been protected by the revolutionary regimes and their successors. The resemblances between the official aesthetics of Stalinism and the officious aesthetics of Mexican politicians and hierarchs are instructive. Mexican mural painting—originally a vigorous movement—was a prime example of this mutual accommodation between the regime and the "progressive" artists. The criticism directed at a showy nationalism and an art of patriotic or revolutionary slogans was more moral than aesthetic: it criticized imposture and servility. This criticism ranged from mural painting (painted oratory) to the verse oratory (mural poetry) that has become something of a vice among many Latin American poets—and not only among the lesser ones: witness the great Neruda. Setting art free was the beginning of a wider freedom.

Their criticism of "revolutionary" and/or patriotic art lead these writers, along with the young

painters, to criticism of the society created by the
Revolution and the epigonic regimes. Again, their
criticism was not and is not direct; it contains no
explicit message and is not inspired by an established doctrine. The form it adopts is neither
moral nor political but exploratory; it is not criticism in the name of this or that principle nor is
it a judgment on reality: *it is a vision*. Criticism
of the language is an active operation that means
digging into the language to discover what is
hidden there: the worm-eaten foundations of institutions, the mire of the subsoil, the slimy crea-
tures therein, the endless underground galleries
like prisons, those Mexican prisons in which so
many of the young are now locked up . . . The
advent of this critical and passionate art, obsessed
with double images of daily marvels and banali-
ties, of humor and passion, surprised and dis-
turbed the new class in power. This was natural
enough. That class, made up of entrepreneurs,
bankers, financiers, and political bosses, is only
now taking its first steps along the path which
their counterparts in Europe and the United States
have been walking for more than a hundred years;
it takes them at precisely the moment when the
nations that have been its models and the object
of its admiration and envy are beginning to suffer
substantial changes in both technology and economics, in both the social sphere and the spiritual,
in both thought and feeling. What is sunrise in

Mexico is sunset there; what is daybreak there is still nothing at all in Mexico. The modernity in which the regime's hierarchs believe is not modern any longer; hence the horror and panic with which they react to the writers and artists, who in their eyes represent those tendencies toward dissolution, criticism, and negation that are undermining the West. The long-kept truce between the intellectuals and those in power, a truce initiated by the Revolution and prolonged by the necessities (the mirage) of development, has now ended. Mexican culture has recovered its vocation as critic of society.

The institutions of higher learning in the capital and the states have been the great centers of political independence during recent years. The ideology and phraseology of Mexico's students and professors reflect those of analogous groups in the United States and Western Europe, but actually their demands reveal an attitude that expresses the aspirations of the new social forces created by the Revolution and industrial development. I am referring in particular to those groups that make up what is called, vaguely enough, the middle class. It contains a good many individuals whose jobs are technical or intellectual in nature; since they are the most active and independent members of their class, they exercise considerable influence over the others. Our middle class is not yet that new class of intellectual workers which the technological society has created in the developed countries, but at the same time it is not the traditional middle class. It constitutes a mobile stratum which, though relatively satisfied from an economic point of view, is aware that the situation could change overnight. This insecurity inspires an aggressiveness and unrest that is not found among the workers, because the latter hold jobs that have been won and then protected by their own unions and the labor laws. In addition to social insecurity, there is another feeling that is no less powerful: the middle class is a product of the post-revolutionary society and no one assigned it a place in the new order of things, with the result that it lacks both an explicit status like that of the proletariat and an implicit status like that of the new bourgeoisie: it has neither union nor club. Finally, it is sensitive to the inequalities it discerns among the functions it performs (considerable), its economic situation (mediocre), and its political influence (nil). All of this explains how it has become the proponent and defender of the desire for democratic change: writers, professors, intellectuals, artists, and students pertain to the middle class. But it has no organization of its own and I doubt if it could create one. Its historic function is not to express itself as a class but to exercise its role as critic in many places and ways, just as it is doing now in the universities, in the groups of workers who serve the state, and even in the labor organizations and the Institutional Revolutionary Party. It is a diffuse national force, active and critical. Because it sows nonconformity and rebelliousness, it is destined to awaken and inspire the other groups and classes to the extent that, in the near future, the persistence of the crisis aggravates the political struggles. These are certain to come, and it is not worth asking whether or not there will be great political battles in Mexico but rather whether they will be public or clandestine, pacific or violent. It is a question that only the regime has the privilege—and the responsibility—of answering.

The Mexican proletariat is not the satisfied and arrogant class that deserted the students in Paris and demonstrated against the blacks in Pittsburgh. Nor is it actively critical and nonconforming like certain sectors of the middle class. Although its material conditions leave a great deal to be desired, its standard of living makes it a privileged group in comparison with the rural population and, in particular, with that immense and wretched floating mass of the semi-unemployed which has emigrated from the countryside to the urban centers. This sector is extremely numerous and its helplessness is almost absolute. Their lack of roots in either the countryside or the city makes all of these ragged, humiliated Mexicans a potential source of rebellion, but they constitute an amorphous group, still bound, though lightly, to the traditional culture, and with rudimentary notions about politics and the world. Nevertheless, it would be a mistake to exaggerate their passivity or scorn their dormant strength. I should say something else about the proletariat: the indifference with which it listens to the radical formulas and watchwords of the young extremists does not imply that it is equally indifferent to the program for democratization. On the contrary: the workers have been dominated and mocked by the corrupt bureaucracies that run the labor unions, bureaucracies which are the strongest pillar of the Institutional Revolutionary Party. I am convinced that one of the regime's most vulnerable points is there in the workers' organizations. The aspirations of the middle class and the working class coincide in this matter: both of them demand greater political participation and a real autonomy. The workers have got to free themselves from their leaders, a caste made up of cynics who have turned their proper function into a business and a politico-bureaucratic career. The political criticism directed at the regime demands, as a first step, the re-establishing of democratic methods within the unions.

Some government spokesmen—journalists, labor and rural leaders, former presidents, and a few ingenuous souls—responded to the student movement by raising two scarecrows: a "Marxist-Leninist" revolution and a military coup. For some, the student revolt was the prelude to a social revolution; for others, a treacherous conspiracy by Yankee imperialism, aimed at provoking a pandemonium that would justify the army's intervention and the liquidation of constitutional order. I note that the army did indeed intervene —to liquidate, not the reigning order, but several hundreds of boys and girls who had gathered in a public place. True, one cannot and should not discount a regression into militarism; I believe, however, that it is not an immediate eventuality. The presidentialist regime and the Institutional Revolutionary Party were created as means of preventing the reoccurrence of military uprisings. If, in the near future, the possibility of a democratic solution to the present crisis is cut off, then the tensions, disorders, and violence would be such that eventually they would open the door to the military; but so far we have not reached that point. The possibility of a social revolution is even more remote. The analysis I have been making throughout these pages excludes the hypothesis of an impending revolution in the cities. The necessary social class, the historical protagonist, is lacking: under present circumstances none of the urban popular sectors combines the conditions that demand revolutionary action. And in the countryside, that other Mexico, the under-developed Mexico? In vast areas of that Mexico there exist the causes which, according to the general idea, produce revolutions. I call the idea "general" because it is one of the extremely few points on which observers on both the right and the left almost always agree. I disagree with both sides, as I will explain.

There is unrest and discontent in the country-side. In many places this unrest has now become exasperation; in other places the discontent is often translated into acts of desperate violence. This is natural: industrialization and develop-ment have been paid for, in great part, by our rural population. While its own very low standard of living scarcely changed, new and relatively prosperous classes, such as the working and mid-dle classes, were created and given the oppor-tunity to increase. For years now, half of Mexico —poorly clothed, illiterate, and underfed—has watched the progress of the other half. Popular violence has broken out here and there, but none of these outbursts was really revolutionary in character: they were, and are, local conflicts. Be-sides, the regime has two weapons of dissuasion: the army and social mobility. The former is odious but real; the latter is a decisive factor, a true safety valve. Because of this social mobility and other circumstances no less positive—distri-bution of lands, irrigation projects, et cetera—it would be absurd to say that the situation in the countryside is revolutionary. It is far from absurd to say that the situation is grievous, but my disagreements with the prophets of rural revolution are not based on economic and social considerations. Agrarian movements (Marx saw this better than anyone) suffer under a double sentence: either they dissipate in a series of local rebellions or they simply halt along the way—whereupon they are destroyed or taken over by other forces that transform them into true revolutions. There is a contradiction of some sort between the exercise of power and the peasant class: there has never been, and there will never be, a peasant state. Peasants have never wanted and do not want to take power; and, when they *have* taken it, they have not known what to do with it. Beginning with Sumer and Egypt there has been an organic relation between the state and the city; the same relation exists, but in the opposite sense of conflict and contradiction, between rural society and the state. Our only link with the Neolithic, that happy age when kings and priests were hardly known, is the countryman.

A clear example of this strong distaste for power—or of this inability to seize it—may be found in 1811, during the movement of Mexican independence, in the actions of Hidalgo and his army of peasants on the outskirts of Mexico City.

They knew that the city was helpless and deserted, but they did not and could not take it; instead, they retreated, and a few months later the army was annihilated and Hidalgo executed. During the Revolution, when the capital was occupied by the forces of Villa and Zapata, the two chieftains visited the National Palace; it is well known that Zapata looked with horror on the presidential chair and, unlike Villa, refused to sit in it. Later he said: "We should have burned it so as to put an end to ambitions." (An observation in passing: the superstitious veneration that is inspired in most Mexicans by the Presidential Chair—the capital letters are *de rigueur* here—is one more indication of the permanence of Aztec and Hispanic-Arabic traits in our make-up. We worship power, and that worship is comprised of terror and adoration: the ambiguous feelings of the lamb as it faces the knife.) Zapata was correct: power corrupts and we should burn every such chair and every throne. Yet, in the inhuman context of history, and especially during a revolutionary period, Zapata's attitude was little different in meaning from Hidalgo's failure to take Mexico City: he that refuses power is condemned, by a fatal process of reversion, to be destroyed by that power. Zapata's visit to the National Palace illustrates the nature of the agrarian movement and its ultimate fate: isolation in the southern mountains, then encirclement, then liquidation at the hands of the Carranza faction. The victories of Carranza and, later, of Obregón and Calles were due to the fact that the three *caudillos,* although they represented conservative tendencies (Carranza in particular), also and above all stood for national aspirations and programs. Villa was dispersion and Zapata was isolation, segregation; the others, once the peasant armies had been beaten, integrated the demands of the rural movement into a larger, a national, program.

Peasants are tied to the land; their viewpoint is not national, much less international; and they conceive of political organizations in traditional terms, which is to say that their models of organization are blood ties, religious ties, and patrimonial ties. When rebellions break out in the countryside they are always local and provincial; if they are to become a revolutionary movement, at least two conditions are indispensable: a central power crisis and the emergence of revolutionary forces capable of transforming isolated rural uprisings into national revolutions. The latter is achieved, in general, through a process that essentially consists in the uprooting of the peasants and their consequent militarization: the countryman is turned into a soldier and the soldier into a revolutionary. This process must coincide with the central power crisis and with the collapse of that power in the cities because of a military defeat (Russia) or an internal conflict together with an external war (China). If these two conditions are not present, the rural rebellion is a mere flare-up that is soon extinguished; Zapata would have been an obscure figure lost in the solitudes of the south if his insurgency had not coincided with the nation's general insurrection and the fall of the Díaz regime in the capital. The case of Cuba also fits the scheme I have just outlined, though with the radical difference that in Cuba there was not even a peasant rebellion: a small army of revolutionaries liquidated a rotten regime, one which at the end lacked all popular support, even that of the bourgeoisie. The theories about guerrilla warfare of the unfortunate Comandante Guevara (intellectual disagreement precludes neither respect nor admiration) were and are a strange renascence of the ideology of Blanqui in the midst of the twentieth century. Strange because unexpected and desperate. But Blanqui at least based his actions on the homogeneity of the urban masses, whereas the theory of guerrilla warfare ignores the heterogeneity between the city and the countryside. Finally, I repeat that if a rural rebellion does not become part of a wider revolutionary process, national in character, it becomes immobilized. The rebellion of the Yellow Turbans, at the close of the Han period in ancient China, was able for years to withstand the combined attacks of the imperial power and the Confucian bureaucracy. The Yellow Turbans were peasant soldiers; they dominated an extensive territory and organized themselves into a communal type of society with tighter and stouter ties than those of any modern ideology: a popular Taoism with a strong magical-religious coloration. All of these circumstances gave them the energy to resist the central power, but not to defeat it; and, since the rebellion could not progress, it became so immobilized that it was surrounded and pitilessly destroyed. The rebellion of the Yellow Turbans did not offer a national alternative. To sum up, then: if a rural uprising is to prosper, it is indispensable that it coincide with a profound power crisis in the cities. In Mexico this conjunction has not come about—not yet.

Three conclusions may be derived from my analysis: first, the crisis in Mexico is the consequence of changes in the social structure and the emergence of new classes—in other words, a crisis of the developed Mexico; second, the country's grave social problems—especially that of integrating the underdeveloped or marginal Mexico into the other—require a democratic solution, one that is truly national in both its domestic and its foreign policies; and, finally, if the regime rejects that democratic solution, the result will not be the *status quo* but rather a state of enforced immobility that will end with an explosion and a return to the old cycle of anarchy and personal dictatorship.

Of course some people will say that this scheme leaves out the other solution, the extreme one—that is, the revolutionary solution. But it depends on what one means by the word "revolution." If one means what the West has meant by it since the birth of the modern age, I have already said elsewhere that in my opinion we are witnessing the end of the epoch of revolutions, at least in the developed countries. And in the underdeveloped countries? No doubt we will see a period of great changes and upheavals, but I am not sure that these transformations will be revolutions in the strictest sense of the word. In fact, I am equally uncertain about the revolutions that took place during the first half of our century. This is more than a semantic quibble. Modern history would seem to demonstrate that there are two kinds of revolutions: on the one hand, those that are the result of historical, economic, social, and cultural development, with the French Revolution as the classical example; and, on the other hand, those that are the result of insufficient development. It is this second kind, I believe, to which the word "revolution" should not be applied. But whatever they are called, it is certain that they are movements which, once they have triumphed, must face the problem of development, and which, to solve it, must sacrifice their other social and political objectives. In this case, revolution is not a result of development but a means of speeding it up. All such revolutions, from the Russian to the Mexican, and whether national or international, degenerate into bureaucratic regimes that are more or less paternalistic and oppressive.

Here I should repeat, at the risk of tedium, that the distinctive feature of the Mexican situation is the existence of a political bureaucracy set up in a state party and composed of specialists in the manipulation of the masses. The Institutional Revolutionary Party, made in the image of Mexico's political and social reality, is a hierarchical bureaucracy, a true pyramid. As I propose to demonstrate in the third part of this essay, that pyramid, besides constituting a social and political reality, also embodies an imaginary reality; the party and the president, without ceasing to be political realities, are mythic projections, forms in which the image we have made of power is condensed. By this, I am not saying that the party is an exclusively Mexican phenomenon, although the myths that nourish it are. I have already noted the universality of the phenomenon and the cause that probably explains it. The emergence of political bureaucracies in the twentieth century may be the consequence of social revolutions in insufficiently developed countries;

the imposition of advanced models of development on archaic societies, and the forced acceleration of the process, explain the institution of regimes of exception. The contradiction between those two words, "institution" and "exception," expresses the basic contradiction, one that is economic in nature but is likewise social and historical. It is frequently forgotten that only a portion of the West—a portion that does not include Spain, Portugal, Latin America, and the majority of the Balkan and Slavic countries, not to mention the cases of Germany and Italy—really possesses the double tradition of political democracy and critical thought, the two central and complementary elements of what we call "modernity."

Modern social thinking did not foresee the emergence of bureaucratic regimes, and until recently it was too disdainful of the phenomenon to analyze it. Both liberals and revolutionaries were possessed by the idea that the state is a secondary reality, devoid of a life of its own, merely the expression of the dominant class or of the fundamental groups that make up a given society. The liberals thought that through democratic controls the state would become weaker and less dehumanized; the Marxists, more radical, asserted that in socialist societies the state would begin to extinguish itself, until it vanished completely on the advent of communism. Not only has the exact opposite occurred, but also we are beginning to suspect that the state is a relatively autonomous reality. We lack a true analysis—that is, an objective and critical analysis—of the modern state. For example: although the Institutional Revolutionary Party is intimately linked to the Mexican bourgeoisie and North American imperialism, it is not a mere agent of either one, and neither of them explains its existence. As for the countries of Eastern Europe: if it is obvious that their Communist parties do not "express" their respective proletariats, what social classes do they "represent"? The theory of the "Asiatic way" of production and the so-called hydraulic theory have been used, with no great success, to explain the ancient Oriental despotisms, all of them characterized by the predominance of immense bureaucracies. But what theory can explain the emergence of bureaucracies in the technological era? In the circles close to Trotsky, during the years immediately preceding his assassination, there was much discussion about the "true nature" of the Soviet state; this led to the elaboration of various hypotheses concerning the function and character of the bureaucracy within that system. Trotsky, loyal to Marx, always denied that the bureaucracy was a class. But what is it, then? Not only have we failed to answer this question, we have not even succeeded in formulating it in a rigorous way. Bureaucracy continues to be a ghostly, elusive concept.

The fusion of the state and what the North Americans call the "military-industrial complex" is one of the most disquieting aspects of the evolution of the capitalist countries. The phenomenon seems to consist in the following: it is not a matter of the domination of the state by financial and economic groups but rather of the emergence of almost institutional formations which, through control of economic, military, and political means, propose a politics of national and/or world domination; and it is not the domination of politics and the state by the financial interests of a minority but rather a monopoly control over the economy and the state by groups and systems in which the interests of politicians, financiers, and the military are indistinguishable. The masks of Hitler and Stalin are now succeeded by an incorporeal reality we cannot even name and execrate. To name it, we have to know it—and only thus can we defeat it. Another surprise: contemporary bureaucratic regimes reject as false the idea that history is a lineal process analogous to the presentation of a thesis—slavery, feudalism, capitalism, et cetera. But this is not the first time that a historical crisis has given rise to a bureaucratic regime: feudal China was succeeded, not by capitalism, but by the system of the mandarins, a caste of learned men who specialized in politics and who governed that country—in an uneasy alliance with the military, the emperor, and other forces—for some two thousand years. The difference is that our modern bureaucracies are not made up of literati. Basically, this is fortunate: one of the extremely few encouraging aspects of the modern situation is that everywhere culture is critical and anti-authoritarian.

None of us knows the shape of the future. This half-century of disorders teaches us that the future is a secret which is divulged neither in the works of Karl Marx nor in those of his adversaries. But we can say this much to the future which a few impassioned young men are somewhere building: every revolution that stifles criticism, that denies the right to contradict those in power, that prohibits the peaceful substitution of one government for another, is a revolution that defeats itself—is a fraud. My conclusions will irritate many people. No matter: independent thought is almost always unpopular. We must renounce outright the authoritarian tendencies of the revolutionary tradition, especially its Marxist branch. At the same time, we must break up the existing monopolies—whether of the state, of parties, or of private capitalism—and discover forms, new and truly effective forms, of democratic and popular control over political and economic power and over the information media and education. A plural society, without majorities or minorities: not all of us are happy in my political utopia, but at least all of us are responsible. Above all and before all else: we must conceive viable models of development, models less inhuman, costly, and senseless than those we have now. I have said before that this is an urgent task: the truth is, *it is the task of our times*. And there is one more thing: the supreme value is not the future but the present. The future is a deceitful time that always says to us, "Not yet," and thus denies us. The future is not the time of love: what man truly wants he wants *now*. Whoever builds a house for future happiness builds a prison for the present.

CRITIQUE
OF THE
PYRAMID

The theme of the two Mexicos, one developed, the other underdeveloped, has appeared here and there throughout these pages. It is the central theme of our modern history, the problem on whose solution our very existence as a people depends. The economists and sociologists generally view the differences between the traditional and the modern society as an opposition between development and underdevelopment: the disparities between the two Mexicos are quantitative in nature and the problem is reduced to the question of whether or not the developed half will be able to absorb the underdeveloped. Now although it is normal for statistics to omit a qualitative description of phenomena, it is hardly normal for our sociologists not to perceive that, behind those figures, there are psychic, historical, and cultural realities which cannot be reflected in the broad measurements the census necessarily must take. Furthermore, those statistical schemes have not been designed for Mexico but are crude adaptations of foreign models. It is one more case of "extralogical imitation," with more of slavish thoughtlessness in it than of scientific rigor. For example, wheat and corn have been chosen as two of the indices of development: the eating of wheat bread is among the signs that one has crossed the line between the underdeveloped and the developed; the eating of corn tortillas indicates that one has not. Two reasons are put forward to justify the inclusion of wheat among the signs of development: it has greater nutritive value and it is a product whose consumption reveals that the leap from a traditional to a modern society has been made. This criterion condemns Japan to eternal underdevelopment, for rice is less nutritive than wheat and is no less "traditional" than corn. Besides, wheat is not really "modern" either, since little distinguishes it from rice and corn except its belonging to a different cultural tradition, that of the West (although the Hindu *chapati* is made of wheat!). So actually the intended meaning is that in all ways, including even diet and cuisine, Western civilization is superior to the others and that, within it, the North American version is the most nearly perfect. Another of the signs of underdevelopment, according to the statisticians, is the use of huaraches. If one thinks in terms of comfort and appearance, then huaraches, in our climate, are superior to shoes; but the fact is that, in the context of our society, corn and sandals are characteristic of the other Mexico.

The developed half of Mexico imposes its model on the other, without noticing that the model fails to correspond to our true historical, psychic, and cultural reality and is instead a mere copy (and a degraded copy) of the North American archetype. Again: we have not been able to create viable models of development, models that correspond to what we are. Up to now, development has been the opposite of what the word means: to open out that which is rolled up, to unfold, to grow freely and harmoniously. Indeed, development has been a strait jacket. It is a false liberation: if it has abolished many ancient, senseless prohibitions, it has also oppressed us with exigencies no less frightening and onerous. It is true that when modern progress arrived, our house, built with the rubble of the pre-Columbian world and the old stones of Spanish-Catholic civilization, was falling apart; but what we have built in its place, a lodging for only a minority of Mexicans, has been deserted by the spirit. The spirit has not gone away, however: it has gone into hiding. When referring to the underdeveloped Mexico, some anthropologists use a revealing expression: "the culture of poverty." The phrase is not so much inexact as insufficient: the other Mexico is poor and in misery; it also is really *other*. This otherness eludes the notions of poverty and wealth, development or backwardness: it is a complex of unconscious attitudes and structures which, far from being survivals from an extinct world, are vital, constituent parts of our contemporary culture. The other Mexico, the submerged and repressed, reappears in the modern Mexico: when we talk with ourselves, we talk with it; when we talk with it, we talk with ourselves.

The division of Mexico into two parts, one of them developed, the other underdeveloped, is scientific and corresponds to our country's economic and social realities. At the same time, on a different stratum there is an *other* Mexico. I am in no way referring to an ahistorical, atemporal entelechy, nor to an archetype in the sense meant by Jung or Mercia Eliade. It is possible that the expression "the other Mexico" lacks precision, but the truth is that I have not been able to find a more appropriate one. By it, I mean that gaseous reality formed by the beliefs, fragments of beliefs, images, and concepts which history deposits in the subsoil of the social psyche, that cave or cellar in continuous somnolence and likewise in perpetual fermentation. It is a notion that derives from both Freud's concept of the subconscious (individual) and the ideology (social) of Marx. An ideology that represents what Marx himself called "the absurd consciousness of the world" and that never is entirely conscious. It seems to me, though, that the concepts of Marx and Freud, each for different reasons which I will not analyze here, do not explain the totality of the phenomenon: the existence in each civilization of certain complexes, presuppositions, and mental structures that are generally unconscious and that stubbornly resist the erosions of history and its changes. Duzèmil calls these structures "ideologies," but in his use of the term he is closer to Kant than to Marx: a certain particular disposition of the mind with regard to objective reality. In short, for me the expression "the other Mexico" invokes a reality that is made up of different strata and that alternately folds in on itself and unfolds, hides itself and reveals itself. If man is double or triple, so are civilizations and societies. Each people carries on a dialogue with an invisible colloquist who is, at one and the same time, itself and the other, its double. Its double? Which is the original and which the phantasm? As with the Moebius strip, there is neither inside nor outside, and otherness is not there, beyond, but here, within: otherness is ourselves. Duality is not something added, artificial, or exterior: it is our constituent reality. Without otherness there is no oneness. And what is more, otherness is oneness made manifest, the way in

which it reveals itself. Otherness is a projection
of oneness: the shadow with which we battle in
our nightmares. And, conversely, oneness is a
moment of otherness, that moment in which we
know ourselves as a body without a shadow—or
as a shadow without a body. Neither within nor
without, neither before nor after: the past reappears because it is a hidden present. I am speaking of the real past, which is not the same as
"what took place": dates, persons, everything we
refer to as history. What took place is indeed in
the past, yet there is something that does not pass
away, something that takes place but does not
wholly recede into the past, a constantly returning present. The history of every people contains
certain invariable elements, or certain elements
whose variations are so slow as to be impercepti-
ble. What do we know of those invariables and
the forms in which they join together or separate?
By analogy with what occurs in other areas, we
can glimpse their mode of operation as the com-
bining of a few elements; as in the case of biological processes, cinematographic montages, or
the verbal associations of poets, those combinations produce distinct and unique figures: that is,
history. But it is deceptive to speak of elements
and invariables as if one were dealing with isolated realities with a life of their own: they always
appear in relation to one another and cannot be
defined as elements but only as parts of a com-

bining. Hence it would not be licit to confuse these complex systems with what are called historical factors, whether economic or cultural. Although those factors are, say, the motor of history, what seems to me decisive, from this perspective, is to determine how they combine: *their form of producing history*. Perhaps the same system of combinations operates among all peoples and in all civilizations—otherwise both the oneness of the human species and the universality of history would be broken—except that in each culture the mode of association is different.

Otherness is what constitutes us. I am not saying by this that the character of Mexico—or of any other people—is unique; I maintain that those realities we call cultures and civilizations are elusive. It is not that Mexico escapes definitions: we ourselves escape them each time we try to define ourselves, to grasp ourselves. Mexico's character, like that of any other people, is an illusion, a mask; at the same time it is a real face. It is never the same and always the same. It is a perpetual contradiction: each time we affirm one part of us, we deny another. That which occurred on October 2, 1968, was simultaneously a negation of what we have wanted to be since the Revolution and an affirmation of what we have been since the Conquest and even earlier. It could be said that it was a manifestation of the other Mexico, or, more precisely, of

one of its aspects. I hardly need to repeat that
the other Mexico is not outside of but within us:
we could not extirpate it without mutilating ourselves. It is a Mexico which, if we learn to name
and recognize it, we can someday bring to an
end by transfiguring it. Then it will cease to be
that phantasm that glides into reality and turns
it into a blood-drenched nightmare. The double
reality of October 2, 1968: it is a historical fact
and it is also a symbolic acting-out of what could
be called our subterranean or invisible history.
And I am mistaken when I call it an acting-out,
because what unfolded before our eyes was a
ritual: a sacrifice. To live history as a rite is our
way of assuming it: if, for the Spaniards, the
Conquest was a *deed,* for the Indians it was a
rite, a human representation of a cosmic catastro-
phe. The sensibilities and imagination of the
Mexican people have always oscillated between
those two extremes, the deed and the rite.

All of the histories of all peoples are symbolic. I mean that history and its events and
protagonists allude to another, occult history,
and are visible manifestations of a hidden reality.
That is why we ask ourselves what the true meaning is of the Crusades, the discovery of America,
the sack of Baghdad, the Jacobin Terror, the
North American War of the Secession. We live
history as if it were a performance by masked
actors who trace enigmatic figures on the stage.

Despite the fact that we know our actions mean something, say something, we do not know what they say and therefore the meaning of the piece we perform escapes us. Does anyone know it? No one can know the final outcome of history because its end is also that of mankind. But we cannot linger over these answerless questions because history obliges us to live it: it is the substance of our life and the place of our death. We pass our lives between living history and interpreting it. In interpreting it, we live it: we make history; in living it, we interpret it: each of our acts is a sign. The history we live is a document, and in this document of our visible history we should read the changes and metamorphoses of our invisible history. This reading is a decipherment, a translation of a translation: we shall never read the original. Each version is provisional: the text changes incessantly (though perhaps it always says the same thing), and so, from time to time, certain versions are discarded in favor of others that in turn had been discarded earlier. Each translation is a creation, a new text. What follows here is an attempt to translate October 2 in terms of what I believe is the true, though invisible, history of Mexico. On that afternoon our visible history unfolded our other history, the invisible one, as if it were a pre-Columbian codex. That vision was shocking because the symbols became transparent.

Geographies, too, are symbolic: physical spaces turn into geometric archetypes that are emissive forms of symbols. Plains, valleys, mountains: the accidents of terrain become meaningful as soon as they enter history. Landscape is historical, and thus becomes a document in cipher, a hieroglyphic text. The oppositions between sea and land, plain and mountain, island and continent, symbolize historical oppositions: societies, cultures, civilizations. Each land is a society: a world and a vision of the world and the otherworld. Each history is a geography and each geography is a geometry of symbols. India is an inverted cone, a tree whose roots are fixed in the heavens. China is an immense disc—belly and navel of the cosmos. Mexico rises between two seas like a huge truncated pyramid: its four sides are the four points of the compass, its staircases are the climates of all the zones, and its high plateau is the house of the sun and the constellations. It is hardly necessary to remind ourselves that to the people of antiquity the world was a mountain and that, in Sumer and Egypt, as in Mesoamerica, the geometric and symbolic representation of the cosmic mountain was the pyramid. The geography of Mexico spreads out in a pyramidal form as if there existed a secret but evident relation between natural space and symbolic geometry and between the latter and what I have called our invisible history.

The Mesoamerican pyramid, archaic archetype of the world, geometric metaphor for the
cosmos, culminates in a magnetic space: the platform-sanctuary. It is the axis of the universe, the
place where the four compass points cross, the
center of the quadrangle: the end and the beginning of motion. An immobility in which the
dance of the cosmos ends and again begins. The
four sides of the pyramid, petrified time, represent the four suns or ages of the world, and its
staircases are days, months, years, centuries. At
the top, on the platform: the birthplace of the
fifth sun, the Nahua and Aztec era. An edifice
made of time: what was, what shall be, what is.
As space, the platform-sanctuary is the place
where the gods appear and the place of the sacri-
ficial altar: the point of convergence of the human world and the divine. As time, it is the center of motion, the end and beginning of the eras:
the everlasting present of the gods. The pyramid is
an image of the world; in turn, that image of the
world is a projection of human society. If it is
true that man invents gods in his own image, it
is also true that he sees his own image in the
images that the sky and the earth offer him. Man
makes human history of the inhuman landscape;
nature turns history into cosmogony, the dance
of the stars.

The pyramid assures the continuity of time
(both human and cosmological) through sacri-

fice: it is a life-generating space. The metaphor
of the world as a mountain and the mountain as
the giver of life materializes with astonishing
literalness in the pyramid. Its platform-sanctuary,
quadrangular like the world, is the theater of the
gods and their playing field. And what is the
game of the gods? They play with time, and
their game is the creation and destruction of
the worlds. There is an opposition between human labors and divine play: man labors in order
to eat, the gods play in order to create. Rather,
there is no difference to them between play and
creation: each of their pirouettes is a world that
is born or annihilated. Creation and destruction
are antithetical notions to man, but identical to
the gods: all is play. In their games—which are
wars which are dances—the gods create, destroy,
and, sometimes, destroy themselves. After their
self-immolation they re-create the world. The
game of the gods is a bloody game culminating
in a sacrifice that is the creation of the world.
The creative destruction of the gods is the model
for man's rites, ceremonies, and fiestas: sacrifice
is equal to productive destruction. To the ancient
Mexicans, *dance* was synonymous with *penitence*. It may seem strange, but it is not: dance
is primordially rite, and rite is ceremony—ceremony that reproduces the gods' creation of the
world in a game that is creative destruction.
There is an intimate connection between divine

play and the gods' sacrifice that engenders the universe; this celestial model has a human counterpart: the ritual dance is penitential.

The dance-penitence equation is repeated in the symbolism of the pyramid: the platform at its summit represents the sacred space where the dance of the gods unfolds, a creative game of motion and thus of time itself. The dancing place, for the same reasons of analogy and correspondence, is also the place of sacrifice. Now, to the Aztecs the world of politics was not distinct from the world of religion: the celestial dance, which is creative destruction, is also cosmic war. This series of divine analogies is repeated in another that is terrestial: the ritual war (or "flower war") is a duplicate of the war dance of the gods and culminates in the sacrifice of prisoners of war. Creative destruction and political domination are the double face, the divine and the human, of a single conception. The pyramid—petrified time, place of divine sacrifice—is also an image of the Aztec state and of its mission: to assure the continuity of the solar cult, source of universal life, through the sacrifice of prisoners of war. The Mexicas* identified themselves with the solar cult: their domination is similar to that of the sun, which daily is born, fights, dies, and is reborn. The pyramid is the

---

* The Aztecs.

world and the world is México-Tenochtitlán: deification of the Aztec capital because of its identification with the ancestral image of the cosmos, the pyramid. To those who inherited the Aztec power, the connection between religious rites and acts of political domination disappears, but, as we shall see, the unconscious model of power is still the same: the pyramid and the sacrifice.

If Mexico is a truncated pyramid, the Valley of Anáhuac is the platform of that pyramid. And in the center of that valley stands Mexico City, the ancient México-Tenochtitlán, seat of Aztec power and today the capital of the Republic of Mexico. As far as I know, it has not been commented on, but there is a special significance in the fact that the capital has given its name to the country. This is a strange thing. Almost everywhere else in the world—the exceptions can be counted on one's fingers—the name of the capital is different from that of the nation. The reason for this, I think, is a universal though unformulated rule: the singular reality of a city must be carefully distinguished from the plural and more extensive reality of a nation. The distinction becomes imperative if, as often happens, the capital is an old metropolis with a history of its own, and, above all, if that history has been one of domination over other cities and provinces: Rome/Italy, Paris/France, Tokyo/Japan,

London/England. Not even the centralists of
Castile dared to break that rule: Madrid/Spain.
The case of Mexico becomes even stranger if one
recalls that, for the peoples who made up the
pre-Hispanic world, the name of México-Tenochtitlán evoked the idea of Aztec domination—I
should say, the terrible reality of that domination. The fact that the whole country was given
the name of the city of its oppressors is one of the
keys to the history of Mexico, her unwritten, un-
spoken history. The fascination that the Aztecs
have exerted has been such that even their con-
querors, the Spaniards, did not escape from it:
when Cortés decided that the capital of the new
kingdom would be built on the ruins of México-
Tenochtitlán, he became the heir and successor
of the Aztecs. Although the Conquest destroyed
the indigenous world and built another and different one on its remains, there is an invisible
thread of continuity between the ancient society
and the new Spanish order: the thread of domination. That thread has not been broken: the
Spanish viceroys and the Mexican presidents are
the successors of the Aztec rulers.

If there has been a secret political continuity
since the fourteenth century, is it any wonder that
the unconscious basis of that continuity is the
religious-political archetype of the ancient Mexicans: the pyramid, the implacable hierarchies,
and, over all, the hierarch and the platform of

sacrifices? When I speak of the unconscious basis of our idea of history and politics, I am thinking, not of those who govern, but of the governed. It is apparent that the Spanish viceroys were unaware of the mythology of the Mexicans, but their subjects were not, whether Indians, mestizos, or Creoles: all of them, naturally and spontaneously, saw the Spanish state as the continuation of Aztec power. This identification was not explicit and never assumed a rational form: it was something that was in the nature of things. Besides, the continuity between the Spanish viceroy and the Aztec lord, between the Christian capital and the ancient idolatrous city, was only one aspect of the idea that colonial society had of the pre-Columbian past. That continuity could also be seen in the realm of religion. The appearance of the Virgin of Guadalupe on the ruins of a shrine sacred to the goddess Tonantzin is the central example, but not the only one, of this relationship between the two worlds, the indigenous and the colonial. In *The Divine Narcissus,* an *auto sacramental* by Sor Juana Inés de la Cruz, the ancient pre-Columbian religion, despite its bloody rites, is shown as a prefiguration of the arrival of Christianity in Mexico. The Spaniards' historical model was Imperial Rome: México-Tenochtitlán and, later, Mexico City were simply reduced versions of the Roman archetype. Christian Rome prolonged, while rectifying, pagan Rome; in the same way, the new Mexico City prolonged, rectified, and in the end affirmed the Aztec metropolis. Independence did not alter this conception radically: it was decided that the Spanish colonial period had been an *interruption* in Mexico's history and that, by freeing itself from foreign domination, the country had re-established its liberties and resumed its traditions. From this point of view, independence was a kind of restoration. This historical-juridical fiction consecrated the legitimacy of Aztec domination: México-Tenochtitlán was and is the origin and source of power. After independence the process of sentimental identification with the pre-Hispanic world became so important that following the Revolution it became one of the most notable characteristics of modern Mexico. What has not been said is that the vast majority of Mexicans has made the Aztec point of view its own and has thus, without knowing it, strengthened the myth that is embodied in the pyramid and the sacrifice stone.

As our knowledge of the Mesoamerican world increases, it changes our attitude toward the Aztecs. For a long time it was thought that pre-Columbian civilization had reached its apogee in México-Tenochtitlán. That was what the Spaniards believed, and it is still believed by a great many Mexicans, not excluding various historians,

archaeologists, art critics, and other students of
our past. But we now know for certain that the
great creative period in Mesoamerica occurred
a number of centuries prior to the arrival of the
Aztecs in the Valley of Anáhuac. It is even probable that Teotihuacán was not Nahua, at least
not exclusively. Hence, though there was an un-
questionable relationship between the culture of
Tula and that of Teotihuacán—the relationship
of a barbarian who inherits and interprets a civilization—it is a mistake to study the totality of
Mesoamerican civilization from the Nahua point
of view (and, worse, from that of its Aztec version), because that totality is older, richer, and
far more diverse. I have discussed this theme
elsewhere at some length.* In any case, the creative phase of Mesoamerica—which today's archaeologists call, I wonder how accurately, the
"period of the great theocracies"—ended in about
the ninth century. The extraordinary artistic and
intellectual fecundity of this period was due, as
I see it, to the coexistence in different parts of
the country of various original cultures (though
possibly they branched from a common bole):
the Mayas, the Zapotecs, the people of Teotihuacán, the people of El Tajín. Instead of the

* "El punto de vista nahua," in *Puertas al campo*
(Mexico City: Universidad Nacional Autónoma de
México, 1966).

hegemony of one state over the others there was diversity and confrontation, that play of influences and reactions on which all creativity finally depends. Mesoamerica was not a pyramid but an assemblage of pyramids. Of course this period was not an epoch of universal peace, as some of our archaeologists have ingenuously called it. Theocracies or not, these city-states were not pacific: the walls of Bonampak commemorate a battle and its ritual corollary, the sacrifice of prisoners, and in Teotihuacán one can see many of the symbols that later figured in the Aztec sun cult, together with the emblems of the military orders of the eagle and the jaguar and various indications of ritual cannibalism. Many scholars minimize these traits of Mesoamerican civilization—a tendency no less harmful than that of those who exaggerate them. Both sides forget that the object of scientific investigation is not to judge but to understand. Besides, Mesoamerica needs neither apologists nor detractors.

The second epoch, which has been called the "historic period," was the epoch of the great hegemonies. It was predominantly Nahua, and began with Tula and its domination over other areas. The Toltecs reached as far as Yucatan, and there the Mayas looked on them with the same wonder and the same horror they later felt in the presence of the Aztecs. To understand the significance of this domination of one people

over another, it is necessary to have seen the
Nahua stone serpent across the front wall of the
temple to the Maya god Chac in Uxmal: it
crosses it and disfigures it like the brand on the
forehead of a slave. Then, after a period of confusion and struggle, Tula's hegemony gave way
to that of México-Tenochtitlán. The new lords,
only recently nomads, had skulked for many years
around the gates of the cities they later con-
quered. The Aztec version of Mesoamerican
civilization was grandiose and somber. The military and religious groups, and also the common
people, were possessed by a heroic and inordinate
belief: that they were the instruments of a sacred
task that consisted in serving, maintaining, and ex-
tending the solar cult and thus helping to preserve
the order of the cosmos. The cult demanded that
the gods be fed human blood in order to keep the
universe operating. A sublime and frightening
idea: blood as the animating substance of the motion of the worlds, a motion analogous to that of
the dance and to that of war. The war dance of the
stars and planets, a dance of creative destruction.
A chain of equations and transformations: rite→
dance→ ritual war→ sacrifice. In this cosmology
the Nahua age and that of its inheritors, the Aztecs, was the fifth age of the world, that of the
fifth sun: the sun of motion, the warrior sun that
drank blood and each day saved the world from
ultimate destruction. Polemical sun, sun of mo-

tion: wars, earthquakes, eclipses, the dance of the cosmos. If the Aztecs were the people of the fifth sun, the end of the world was related to the end of Aztec supremacy; hence the avoiding of both, through wars, the enslavement of other nations, and sacrifices, would be a sacred task as well as a political-military enterprise. That identification of a cosmic era with their own national destiny is the most notable aspect of the overlapping of the Aztecs' religious and philosophical ideas and their political interests. One of Sahagún's native informants explained in a memorable way the true religious significance of Huitzilopochtli, national god of the Mexicas: *The god is us*. Not "the people is god," as with Western democrats, but *the god is the people:* divinity is incarnate in society and imposes on it inhuman tasks, those of sacrificing and being sacrificed. The "Aztec peace," as the Mexicas' hegemony has been called by one of its erudite contemporary idolaters, made ritual warfare a permanent institution: the vassal peoples, such as those of Tlaxcala, were periodically obliged to celebrate pitched battles with the Aztecs and their allies so as to provide them (and themselves) with prisoners to be sacrificed. The subject nations constituted a reserve of sacred sustenance. The "flower war" combined the hunt and the tourney with a modern philanthropic institution: the blood bank.

The Aztecs modified their national religious tradition in order to adapt it to an earlier cosmology created by the Toltecs or, perhaps, by the people of Teotihuacán itself. The tribal god, Huitzilopochtli, "the Warrior of the South," was at the center of the cult; at his side were the great gods of the cultures that had preceded the Aztecs in the Valley of Anáhuac: Tláloc, Quetzalcóatl. Thus they confiscated a singularly profound and complex vision of the universe to convert it into an instrument of domination.* Solar religion and expansionist ideology, superhuman heroism and inhuman political realism, sacred madness and cold astuteness—such were the extremes between which the Aztec ethos moved. This psychic and moral duality was in correlation with the dualism of their social organization and with that of their religious and cosmological thought. Upon this dualism—a distinctive trait of the Nahuas and perhaps a characteristic of all American Indians—there was superimposed another of a historical nature: an amalgamation of the beliefs of the sedentary peoples of the Central Plateau with those of the nomads which the Aztecs had been. A solar religion and an agricultural religion, Jacques Soutelle has remarked. This religious

---

* Various authors have written studies on this topic; among the most recent and perceptive are those by Laurette Séjourné.

and cosmological syncretism corresponded, on
the one hand, to the moral duplicity I mentioned
earlier and, on the other, to a hybrid art that
varied between the sublime and the grotesque,
between the monotony of the official style and
an art that combined fierce life with intellectual
rigor, passion, and geometry. Our art critics wax
ecstatic about the statue of Coatlicue, an enormous block of petrified theology. Have they ever
looked at it? Pedantry and heroism, sexual puritanism and ferocity, calculation and delirium: a
people made up of warriors and priests, astrolo-
gers and immolators. And of poets, too: that
world of brilliant colors and somber passions was
crisscrossed with lightning flashes of poetry. And
in all the manifestations of that extraordinary
and horrifying nation, from the astronomical
myths to the poets' metaphors, from the daily
rites to the priests' meditations, there is always
the smell of blood, the obsessive reek of it. The
Aztec year, like those wheels-of-torture circles
that appear in the novels of Sade, was a circle of
eighteen blood-soaked months, eighteen ceremonies, eighteen ways of dying: by arrows, by
drowning, by beheading, by flaying . . . Dance
and penitence.

What religious and social aberration caused
a city as beautiful as México-Tenochtitlán—
water, stone, and sky—to be the scene of a hallu-
cinatory and funereal ballet? And what obfusca-

tion of the spirit is responsible for that fact that no one among us—I am speaking, not of our outdated nationalists, but of our philosophers, historians, artists, poets—wishes to see and to admit that the Aztec world was one of history's aberrations? The case of the Aztecs is unique because their cruelty was the result of a system impeccably and implacably coherent, an irrefutable syllogism-dagger. That violence can be explained as the result of sexual puritanism, repression of the senses, and the crushing weight of religion; but what stuns and paralyzes the mind is the use of realistic means in the service of a metaphysic both rigorously rational and delirious, the insensate offering up of lives to a petrified concept. It was not the homicidal rage of Genghis Khan and Tamerlane nor the White Huns' intoxicated delight in killing and burning. Instead, the Mexicas are reminiscent of the Assyrians, and not only because of the splendor of their capital and the grandiose and liturgical nature of their slaughters: the Assyrians, too, were inheritors of a high culture and were equally partial to the truncated pyramid (the ziggurat). But the Assyrians were not theologues. In fact, the real rivals of the Aztecs are not to be found in the East at all but rather in the West, for only among ourselves has the alliance between politics and metaphysics been so intimate, so exacerbated, and so deadly: the inquisitions, the religious wars, and, above all, the totalitarian societies of the twentieth century. I do not presume, of course, to judge the Aztec world, and still less to condemn it. México-Tenochtitlán has disappeared, and what concerns me, as I gaze upon its fallen body, is not the problem of historical interpretation but the fact that we cannot contemplate the cadavar face to face: its phantasm inhabits us. For this reason I believe that a critique of Mexico and its history—a critique resembling the therapeutics of the psychoanalysts—should begin by examining what the Aztec world view meant and still means. The image of Mexico as a pyramid is one viewpoint among many others equally possible: the viewpoint of what is on the platform at its top. It is the viewpoint of the ancient gods and of those who served them, the Aztec lords and priests. It is also that of their heirs and successors: the viceroys, the generals, the presidents. And, furthermore, it is the viewpoint of the vast majority, of the victims crushed by the pyramid or sacrificed on its platform-sanctuary. The critique of Mexico begins with the critique of the pyramid.

Mesoamerica's second epoch, as I have said, was that of Tula and México-Tenochtitlán. Both states weighed down upon the other peoples like those gigantic stone warriors the archaeologists have excavated in the first of those cities. Repetitions, amplifications, immense works, inhuman grandeur—but nothing comparable to the great creative period. What I want to emphasize, however, is the relationship of the Aztecs with the Mesoamerican tradition. It is known that they were wholly or almost wholly ignorant about the "great theocracies" that had preceded Tula. I must confess that their ignorance makes me shudder: it was the same as that of the Dark Ages regarding Greco-Roman civilization, the same as that of our descendants someday regarding Paris, London, New York. If the Aztecs' notions about Teotihuacán and its builders were rudimentary and grotesque, their notions about Tula were toplofty. They always claimed, with enormous pride, that they were the direct and legitimate heirs of the Toltecs, that is, of Tula and Culhuacán. To understand the reason for their pretension one must remember that for the Aztecs the universal dichotomy *civilized/barbarian* was expressed by the terms *Toltec/Chichimec*. The Aztecs wanted to forget their Chichimec (barbarian) past. This pretension had little basis: before the founding of México-Tenochtitlán they had been a band of fugitives beyond the pale. The feeling of illegitimacy, common to all barbarians and newcomers, was like a wound in the Aztecs' psyche; it was also a defect in their credentials as rulers of the world by the will of Huitzilopochtli. In fact, Huitzilopochtli, supposed center of the fifth-sun cosmology and support of the solar cult, was only a tribal god, an upstart among the ancient divinities of Mesoamerica. That is why the Aztec ruler Itzcóatl, with the counsel of the celebrated Tlacaélel, architect of Mexica grandeur, ordered that the ancient codices and documents be burned and that new ones be fabricated, the purpose of the latter being to "prove" that the Aztecs were the descendants of the lords of Anáhuac. By affirming their direct relationship with the Toltec world, the Aztecs also affirmed the legitimacy of their hegemony over the other nations of Mesoamerica. This makes clearer the correlation between their falsifying of history and their religious syncretism.

The subject nations looked on these doctrines skeptically. The Aztecs themselves knew that a fraud had been perpetrated, but none of them dared to admit it, even to himself. All this explains why Montezuma II, receiving Cortés, greeted him as the envoy of someone who was claiming his inheritance. I want to make it clear that he did *not* receive him as an emissary of the Emperor Charles, but rather as a god (or semigod or warlock-warrior—the Aztecs never succeeded in formulating definite ideas about the nature of the Spaniards) who had been sent to re-establish the sacred order of the fifth sun, which had been interrupted by the fall of Tula. The Spaniards' arrival coincided with an interregnum in Mesoamerica. The destruction of Tula and the flight of Quetzalcóatl (god-chieftain-priest), who prophesied that one day he would come back, had been followed by the hegemony of México-Tenochtitlán; but the Aztecs, because of their barbarian origins, were perpetually threatened by the return of those who truly embodied the principle of the fifth sun, that is, the legendary Toltecs. The attitude of the Mesoamerican world toward the Spaniards is still more understandable when one recalls that, according to legend, the priest-king Topiltzin Quetzalcóatl was born in the year 1-Ácatl (cane) and that his flight and disappearance took place fifty-two years later, again in the year 1-Ácatl. It was generally believed that Quetzalcóatl would return in another 1-Ácatl year—and Cortés arrived in Mexico in 1519, again 1-Ácatl! The speech with which Montezuma greeted Cortés is remarkable: "My lord, you are tired, you are weary; you have now come back to your land. You have arrived in your city, Mexico. You have come to sit on your throne, under its canopy. Oh, brief was the while they held it for you, preserved it for you, those who have gone before, your substitutes." The Aztec sovereign did not question the Spaniard's divine credentials; Mexico belonged to Cortés, not by right of conquest but because of his original property rights: he had come to recover his inheritance. And Montezuma specifi-

cally said that "those who have gone before"—
by which he meant his predecessors, the former
rulers of Mexico: Itzcóatl, Montezuma I, Tizoc,
Axayácatl, Ahuítzotl—governed only as *substitutes,* as regents. Like Montezuma himself, they
were nothing more than the guardians, the cus-
todians, of the Toltec legacy. Montezuma pointed
out—I am not sure whether in sadness or in an
attempt to win favor with Cortés—that the re-
gency lasted for only a short spell: "Oh, brief was
the while they held it for you . . ." And there
is pathos in his insistence: "I was in agony for
five days, for ten days, with my eyes fixed on the
Region of Mysteries. And you have come, among
clouds, among mists. For that is what our kings
had foretold, those who reigned, those who governed your city: that you would assume your
throne, that you would come here." * But I cannot give more time to an analysis of this theme.
One could spend a whole lifetime studying and
explaining the Conquest.

This attitude of Montezuma and the ruling
class of México-Tenochtitlán is not so fantastic
as it seems at first glance: the return of Tula and
Quetzalcóatl fitted naturally into a circular conception of time. The idea disturbs us because we

---

* Miguel León-Portilla, ed., *Visión de los vencidos*
(Mexico City: Universidad Nacional Autónoma de
México).

are moderns, at once the devotees and victims of
the different conception that progress imposes on
us: we think of time as being rectilinear and un-
repeatable, and cannot accept the idea of cyclical
time and its many consequences. In the case of
the Aztecs, the idea of time returning was rooted
in a feeling of guilt: earlier time, on returning,
assumed the form of a *reparation*. This would
not have been possible if the Aztecs had not felt
guilty about Tula's mythic past and their own
domination over other peoples. The proof of this
is the strange episode of the god Tezcatlipoca's
appearance. We know that this god played a decisive role in the fall of Tula. Like Satan with
Christ and Mara with Buddha, Tezcatlipoca was
Quetzalcóatl's tempter—except that, being luck-
ier and cleverer, he succeeded through sorcery
in inducing that ascetic god to get drunk and
then to commit incest with his sister. The ruina-
tion of both Quetzalcóatl and his city was the
result.

Tezcatlipoca was especially venerated by
the Mexicas. Therefore, when Montezuma II
learned that Cortés and his soldiers—deaf to
pleas, deaf to veiled threats—had refused to turn
back and were continuing to march toward
México-Tenochtitlán, the Aztec ruler decided to
oppose them with the one infallible weapon: sorcery. He sent out a group of warlocks and magicians, but just as they were about to reach the

Spaniards they ran across a young man "who
spoke as if he were drunk" (possessed by divine
madness?) and who halted them to say: "What
is it you want? What is Montezuma trying to do?
. . . He has committed errors . . . he has destroyed people." The warlocks listened intently
to the confused and muttered words of the young
"drunkard." When they tried to touch him, he
vanished. Yet they still heard his voice, which
told them to look behind, toward the valley
where the capital stood. "The temples were on
fire, and so were the communal halls and the religious schools and all the houses of the city. And
it was as if a great battle were raging. And when
the warlocks saw this, their hearts fled away
from them. Now they could not speak clearly
. . . They said, 'He was not an anybody, he
was the young Tezcatlipoca!' " The magicians
returned without having accomplished their mission and told Montezuma what they had seen
and heard. At first he was so dejected that he said
nothing, but at last he murmured: "What help
is there now, my stalwarts? . . . With this they
have given us fit punishment!" * To Montezuma
the arrival of the Spaniards meant, in a way, the
paying of an old debt, incurred by the Aztecs'
sacrilegious usurpation. Their mingling of religion and politics had served the Aztecs well as

---

* Cf. *Visión de los vencidos*.

a justification of their hegemony, but it became
a liability once the Spaniards arrived: the divinity
of the latter had the same origin as the purported
cosmic mission of the Aztec people. Both were
agents of the divine order, representatives and
instruments of the fifth sun. The strangest aspect
of the situation is that the Spaniards had no ink-
ling of how complex the Indians' attitudes toward
them really were. And there was another element
that further increased the tragic confusions these
errors created: the Spaniards' Indian allies hoped
that the fall of México-Tenochtitlán would put
an end to the interregnum, the usurpation, and
their own vassalage. Perhaps their horrible dis-
illusionment was the cause of their centuries-long
passivity: the Spaniards, on making themselves
the successors of the Aztecs' rule, also perpetu-
ated their usurpation.

As the heirs of México-Tenochtitlán, the
Spaniards became the transmitters of the Aztec
archetype of political power: the *tlatoani,* or
ruler, and the pyramid. The transmission was involuntary and, for that reason, incontrovertible:
an unconscious transmission, exempt from rational examination and criticism. During the
course of our history the Aztec archetype has
sometimes opposed, sometimes become fused
with, the Hispanic-Arabic archetype, which is the
caudillo. This oscillation between the *tlatoani* and

the *caudillo* is one of the traits that differentiate us from Spain, Portugal, and most of the other Latin-American countries,* where *caudillismo* reigns without a rival. The *tlatoani* is impersonal, priestly, and institutional—hence the abstract figure of the president corresponds to a bureaucratic and hierarchic corporation like the Institutional Revolutionary Party. The *caudillo* is personal, epic, and exceptional—hence he makes his appearance when the normal order of affairs is upset. The *tlatoani* represents an impersonal continuation of the rule, while a caste of priests and hierarchs exercises power during its successive incarnations. The president *is* the Party during his six-year term; but, when it ends, another president appears, and is only another incarnation of the Party. Different and the same: the double exigency of Mexico's presidential institution. The power concentrated in the president's hands is enormous, but it never is personal power, it is instead a consequence of his impersonal investiture. The *caudillo* belongs to no caste and is not selected by any governing body, sacred or profane: he is an unexpected presence who appears in times of crisis and confusion, rules until the storm blows itself out, and then vanishes as suddenly as he appeared. The *caudillo* governs behind the back of the law: he

---

* The exceptions are Chile, Uruguay, and Costa Rica.

makes the law. The *tlatoani*—whether his power derives from the Aztecs' usurpation or the Party's monopoly—always takes refuge in legality: whatever he does is done in the name of the law.

We have had many a *tlatoani* and many a *caudillo* in our history: Juárez and Santa Ana, Carranza and Villa. None of them has been completely the one or the other, of course, but there is a clue that reveals the secret supremacy of the Aztec model: all of the leaders we have had, even the most arbitrary and *caudillo*-like, have aspired to the category of *tlatoani*. There is a Mexican nostalgia for legality that other Spanish-American *caudillos* do not feel; all of them—whether one considers Bolívar and Fidel Castro or Rosas and Juan Perón—have believed and believe that an act is a deed, whereas Mexicans affirm that the same act is a rite. In the one case, violence is transgression; in the other, expiation. The founding of the National Revolutionary Party initiated the decline of Mexican *caudillismo*; at the same time, the Aztec archetype became more and more solidly consolidated. It could not have been otherwise: that archetype is the very model of stability, and, after some twenty years of civil war and of violent quarrels among the revolutionary *caudillos,* stability is the political value that Mexico most desires and appreciates. But the partisans of stability *à outrance* forget a circumstance that upsets the whole pyra-

midal edifice, however solid it may appear: the
Institutional Revolutionary Party was conceived
as a solution to the problems of exception and
transition, so that the continuation of its political monopoly has a certain analogy with the
usurpation committed by México-Tenochtitlán
and with that city's pretension that it was the
axis of the fifth sun. The translation of pre-
Hispanic mythical concepts into contemporary
political terms does not end, however, with the
equivalence between the Party's usurpation of
the revolutionary heritage and the Aztecs' usurpation of the Toltec heritage. The fifth sun—
the era of motion, of earthquakes, of the collapse of the great pyramid—corresponds to the
historical period in which the whole world now
lives: revolts, rebellions, and other social upheavals. We will not be rescued from the agi-
tations and convulsions of the fifth sun by the
stability, solidity, and hardness of stone but rather
by lightness, flexibility, and capacity for change.
Stability leads to petrification, to the stone mass
of the pyramid, which the sun of motion shatters
and grinds to dust.

The plaza of Tlatelolco is magnetic with
history. Tlatelolco itself, an expression of Mesoamerican dualism, was actually a twin center with
México-Tenochtitlán. Although it never lost its
autonomy entirely, it lived in strict dependence

on the dominant power after an attempt at rebellion had been harshly put down by the *tlatoani*
Axayácatl. It was the seat of the merchant class,
and its great plaza contained not only temples
but also a celebrated market that Bernal Díaz
and Cortés have described with detailed and enchanted exaltation, as if they were recounting a
legend. During the siege, Tlatelolco resisted the
Spaniards tenaciously and was the last Aztec
stronghold to surrender. Then, in the midst of
that immense stone esplanade, the evangelizers
—as if laying a risky bet—planted (it is the only
word) a minuscule church. It is still standing.
Tlatelolco is one of Mexico's roots: there the
missionaries taught classical literature, Spanish
literature, rhetoric, philosophy, and theology to
the Aztec nobles; there Sahagún founded the
study of pre-Hispanic history. The crown and
the church brutally interrupted these studies, and
both Mexicans and Spaniards are still paying the
consequences of that deadly interruption: Spain
isolated us from our Indian past and thus isolated herself from us. Afterward, Tlatelolco lived
an obscure life: military prison, railroad yards,
dusty suburb. A few years ago the regime transformed the area into a complex of huge low-rent
apartment buildings, and in doing so wanted to
rescue the venerable plaza: it discovered part of
the pyramid and, in front of it and the minuscule
church, built an anonymous skyscraper: the Min-

istry of Foreign Affairs. The conjunction is not a happy one: three excesses in an urban desolation. The name chosen for the plaza was that platitude of Columbus Day speakers: Plaza of the Three Cultures. But nobody uses the official name; everybody calls it Tlatelolco. This preference for the ancient Mexican name is not accidental: October 2, Tlatelolco, inserts itself with terrifying logic in our history, both the real and the symbolic.

Tlatelolco is the counterpart, in terms of blood and sacrifice, of the petrification of the Institutional Revolutionary Party. Both are projections of the same archetype, although with different functions within the implacable dialectic of the pyramid. It is as if contemporary facts were a metaphor for that past which is a buried present: the relation between the ancient plaza of Tlatelolco and the main plaza of México-Tenochtitlán is now repeated in the connection between the new Plaza of the Three Cultures and the Zócalo.* The relation between these two places is explicit if one considers our visible history, but it also becomes symbolic when one recognizes that it alludes to what I have called the invisible history of Mexico. True, we can

---

* The main plaza of Mexico City, built on the ruins of that of México-Tenochtitlán. It contains both the Cathedral of Mexico and the National Palace.

shrug our shoulders and reject any interpretation that goes beyond what the newspapers and the statistics tell us. But to reduce the significance of a fact to our visible history is to deny oneself real comprehension and, indeed, to submit to a kind of spiritual mutilation. To make clear the true character of the relation between the Zócalo and Tlatelolco we must turn to a third landmark and question another place no less magnetic with history: Chapultepec Park. The regime has constructed a proud monument there, the National Museum of Anthropology. If Mexico's visible history is the symbolic script of its invisible history and if both are the expression, reiteration, and metaphor—on different levels of reality—of certain repressed and submerged moments, it is evident that in this museum we can find, even though in dispersed fragments, the elements that can serve us to reconstruct the figure we seek. But the museum offers us something more—and something more immediate, tangible, and obvious—than the broken symbols and excavated stones its halls contain: in both the museum itself and in the spirit that animates it the archetype is at last completely unveiled. In fact, the image it presents us of Mexico's past obeys not so much the exigencies of science as the aesthetics of the paradigm. It is not a museum, it is a mirror—except that in its symbol-crammed surface we do not reflect ourselves but instead

contemplate the giganticized myth of México-
Tenochtitlán with its Huitzilopochtli and his
mother Coatlicue, its *tlatoani* and Serpent-
Woman, its prisoners of war and hearts-as-fruits.
In that mirror we do not see deep into our own
image: we adore the image that is crushing us.

To enter the Museum of Anthropology is
to penetrate an architecture built of the solemn
matter of myth. There is an enormous rectangular
patio, and in that patio there is a great parasol
from which light and water fall with a sound of
broken calendars—a rain of years and centuries
splashing on the gray-green stones. The parasol
is supported by a stone column that would be
impressive if it were not covered with reliefs that
repeat the themes of the official rhetoric. But it
is ethics, not aesthetics, that prompts me to speak
of the museum: in it, anthropology and history
have been made to serve an idea about Mexico's
history, and that idea is the foundation, the buried
and immovable base, that sustains our concep-
tions of the state, of political power, and of social
order. The visitor strolls enchanted through hall
after hall: the smiling Neolithic world with its
little nude figures; the Mayas, miners of time
and the heavens; the Huastecos with their great
stones whose carving has the simplicity of line
drawings; the culture of El Tajín, an art that
escapes both "Olmec" heaviness and the hierar-
chism of Teotihuacán without falling into Mayan

baroque, being instead a wonder of feline grace;
and the Toltecs with their tons and tons of
sculpture—all the diversity and complexity of
two thousand years of Mesoamerican history pre-
sented as a prologue to the last act, the apothe-
osis-apocalypse of México-Tenochtitlán. I hardly
need to point out that, from the viewpoint of
science and history, the image of the pre-Columbian past which the Museum of Anthropology
offers us is false. In no way do the Aztecs represent the culmination of the diverse cultures that
preceded theirs. Indeed, the contrary is true: their
version of Mesoamerican civilization simplifies
it on the one hand and exaggerates it on the
other, and in both ways it impoverishes it. This
exaltation and glorification of México-Tenochtitlán transforms the Museum of Anthropology
into a temple. The cult propagated within its
walls is the same one that inspires our school-
books on Mexican history and the speeches of
our leaders: the stepped pyramid and the sacri-
ficial platform.

Why have we sought Mexico's archetype
among those pre-Hispanic ruins? And why must
that archetype be only Aztec and not Mayan or
Zapotec or Tarascan or Otomí? My answer to
these questions will not please a lot of people:
the true heirs of the pre-Columbian world are
not the peninsular Spaniards but ourselves, we
Mexicans who speak Spanish, whether we are

Creoles, mestizos, or Indians. Thus the museum expresses a feeling of guilt—except that, by a process of transference and unburdening which psychoanalysis has often studied and described, the guilt is transfigured into a glorification of the victim. At the same time—and this is what seems to me decisive—its ultimate exaltation of the Aztec period confirms and justifies what in appearance condemns the museum: the survival, the continuing strength, of the Aztec model of domination in our contemporary history. I have already said that the relationship between the Aztecs and the Spaniards was not only one of opposition: Spanish power took the place of Aztec power and thus continued it. Independent Mexico, in its turn, explicitly and implicitly prolonged the centralist, authoritarian, Aztec-Spanish tradition. I repeat: there is a bridge that reaches from *tlatoani* to viceroy, viceroy to president. The glorification of México-Tenochtitlán in the Museum of Anthropology is an exaltation of the image of the Aztec pyramid, now guaranteed, so to speak, by science. The regime sees itself, transfigured, in the world of the Aztecs. And in contemplating itself it affirms itself. Therefore a critique of Tlatelolco, the Zócalo, and the National Palace—a political, social, and moral critique—includes the Museum of Anthropology and is also a historical critique. If politics is a dimension of history, a critique of history is likewise political and moral criticism. We must oppose the Mexico of the Zócalo, Tlatelolco, and the Museum of Anthropology, not with another image—all images have a fatal tendency to become petrified—but with criticism, the acid that dissolves images. In this case (and perhaps in others), criticism is but one of the imagination's ways of working, one of its manifestations. In our age the imagination operates critically. True, criticism is not what we dream of, but it teaches us to distinguish between the specters out of our nightmares and our true visions. Criticism is the imagination's apprenticeship in its second turn, the imagination cured of fantasies and determined to face the world's realities. Criticism tells us that we should learn to dissolve the idols, should learn to dissolve them within our own selves. We must learn to be like the air, a liberated dream.

POSTSCRIPT

Late in 1971 Adolfo Gilly's *La revolución interrumpida* (*The Interrupted Revolution*) was
published in Mexico. The book is an interpretation of the Mexican revolutionary movement
(1910–1920), and in the final chapter the author
discusses the situation in Mexico today. Adolfo
Gilly is an author with Trotskyist tendencies, and
his book was written in Lecumberri Prison in
Mexico City. He was recently liberated, as most
political prisoners of the previous regime have
been in accordance with the policy of *"apertura
democrática"* ("democratic liberalization") an-
nounced by the present President of Mexico, Luis
Echeverría. The letter below, from Octavio Paz
to Gilly, completes *The Other Mexico* and brings
it up to date. This letter was published in the
monthly review *Plural* (no. 5, 15 de febrero,
1972).

LETTER TO ADOLFO GILLY

Cambridge, Massachusetts, January 19, 1972

Sr. Adolfo Gilly
Lecumberri Prison, Wing N
Mexico, D. F.

The letter you sent me has only just now reached me. I am not living in Mexico at present, having left in October (though I will be back in a few months). Moreover, your publisher failed to send me your book, *La revolución interrumpida*. Fortunately, a friend lent me a copy a few days ago. I read it from beginning to end without once putting it down. It is a remarkable contribution to the history of the Mexican Revolution, and an equally remarkable contribution to living history, that is to say, the history we are all living and making (and, at times, unmaking) in Mexico these days. You have pointed out a great many new things, reminded us of others that we had forgotten, and shed light on still others that had seemed obscure to us. Nonetheless I shall tell you frankly that I disagree with many of your statements. Since my intention is not to write a study of your book—although it more than deserves such a study—but rather to exchange views with you, I shall here limit myself to commenting on the final section, the one bearing most directly on the present situation, in order to outline briefly

the specific points on which I agree and disagree
with you.

We all know that we have been undergoing
a historic crisis in Mexico for a number of years
now. I quite agree with you that any attempt to
resolve this crisis must begin with a return to the
Cárdenas tradition, despite the fact that the national and international situation is very different
today. This return to the Cárdenas tradition must,
naturally, be merely the starting point rather than
the ultimate goal. The great lesson of Cárdenism,
its meaning for us today, lies in the fact that it
set an example of what a great popular coalition
can be and continually reminds us of the historical and social possibilities of a movement of this
sort. At the same time, it teaches us that such a
popular coalition must remain independent of the
state and the Party, something that was not possible in the Cárdenas era.

I also agree with what you say about the
three great achievements of the Mexican Revolution, which are still vital forces despite the fact
that they have been distorted: the *ejido* (common
public land), nationalized enterprises, and labor
unions. These achievements must not only be de-
fended but adapted to our present circumstances,
and above all we must see to it that they regain
their original social function. The low prices of
nationalized petroleum, for example, have served
above all else as a subsidy to industrialists rather

than a stimulus for the creation of a good collective system of transportation. The conquests of the Mexican people, which have fallen into the hands of the bourgeoisie and been used for their profit alone, must be resocialized. The fanatical splinter groups who scorn this heritage and are eager to begin all over again from nothing are doomed to suffer a fate worse than the Communists in the Cárdenas era. Back then the Communists turned out to be the caboose in the Cárdenist train; today splinter groups are becoming a tiny little twilight orchestra of frogs and crickets striking up mad little tunes on the outskirts of reality. The monotonous theme of this dissonant musical score is "revolution now," but its real meaning, what psychoanalysts call the *latent content,* is political suicide.

The popular coalition should include farm laborers and small agriculturists, as well as those living on *ejidos;* employees of nationalized enterprises; and workers. Other groups which you mention only in passing should also be included: technicians, students, teachers, intellectuals, workers in the tertiary sector, and other middle-class groups. The appearance of these groups in public life—and indeed their every existence—is one of the consequences of the economic development of the last thirty years. It is therefore not surprising that they have been the first to express their discontent with the present state of affairs in an articulate manner. They have also been the first to voice the aspirations of the people as a whole, if only in a confused way, as was clearly demonstrated by the events in 1968. As for technicians: I would like to stress the fact that both within the nationalized enterprises and within the state, they have traditionally been the defenders of the revolutionary heritage, against national capitalism and imperialism alike. And finally, you also fail to mention the enormous numbers of rural peasants who have emigrated to the cities, where they live on the margin of society, barely able to subsist. I call them "urban nomads," although real nomads take their culture and their institutions with them wherever they go whereas these unfortunates who have been uprooted from their world and deprived of everything they once had have been flung into the urban vacuum. Their real homeland is a vacant lot. Precisely because of this material poverty and this loss of their traditions, these groups may become instruments of reactionary violence. [Isn't this in fact the social background of Los Halcones (The Falcons) and other para-military gangs?]* Nonetheless, a popular coalition could change the picture entirely: if they were given a place within a vast movement of national recovery, the road leading to the at-

---

* A para-military group which attacked and routed a group of demonstrating students, causing several deaths, on June 10, 1971.

tainment of a social and psychic identity would be open to them. The road leading back to one's true self passes by way of others . . . But in the final analysis, I believe that despite our differences on the subject, we both agree that it is necessary and *possible* to form a great independent coalition front.

I must now touch on another subject: the causes of the present crisis and the reasons for popular unrest. Here too the example of the Cárdenist period will help us understand the current situation. In your analysis of the causes of the great shift in public opinion that put Cárdenas in office, you mention the following factors: the anti-imperialist and Socialist tendencies of an active (though vastly outnumbered) group within the PNR and the government (systematically ignored by the Stalinist Communists); the growing number of workers' strikes; the situation in rural areas, where people were frustrated because agrarian reform had slowed to a virtual halt and there had been frequent outbreaks of violence. It would seem to me that you are forgetting Vasconcelism.* Whatever its confusions and its errors, that movement fulfilled an important political function, if only a negative one: it vigorously

---

* A political movement founded in 1929 and headed by the writer José Vasconcelos. Most of its support came from students, intellectuals, and the middle class.

criticized Callism* on moral grounds, it de-
nounced the corruption of revolutionaries who
had made ill-gotten fortunes, and it tore off the
democratic mask that the regime was hiding behind. Callism lost whatever moral authority it
still had (it had already been rather seriously
undermined following Obregón's assassination).
The Cárdenist renaissance can be explained by
the following conjuncture of circumstances: the
existence of a left wing within the PNR and the
government; the social energy unleashed by the
reforms instituted by Obregón and by Calles in
his early days, which continued to accumulate
during the period of repression and began to
manifest itself around 1933 in a series of uprisings by workers and peasants; and the gradual
moral decay of Callism.

In your analysis of the international situation during this period, you stress the fact that
in other parts of the world there were more or
less similar movements, such as the populism of
the early years of Roosevelt's presidency and the
Popular Fronts. On the other hand, you perhaps
minimize certain factors that would appear to
have been entirely adverse ones, such as Fascism
and the rise of Hitler. The point that I am at-
tempting to make is that there was a great diver-

---

* The regime of Plutarco Elias Calles, the "Maximum Leader of the Revolution." Calles's political
rule was ended by Lázaro Cárdenas in 1936.

sity and multiplicity of tendencies in this period, by comparison with the great uniformity during the period following the Second World War. One of your statements strikes me as a mere figment of your imagination: "The nationalist revolution in Mexico was able to go as far as it did during the Cárdenist phase because even though it was hemmed in by imperialism, the Soviet Union existed, and despite the policies of its leaders, it was a source of objective support for progressive revolutionary movements of the masses all over the world" (page 352). I confess that I fail to see how, where, or when the Soviet Union was ever "a source of *objective* support" for the Mexican movement. Could you offer any concrete example? In actual fact, the international situation favored Cárdenas's policy for an essential reason which you neglect to mention and which has nothing, or very little, to do with the struggles of the international proletariat: the quarrels between the great powers. Only in a world divided into various camps—the United States, Great Britain and France, Germany and Italy, the Soviet Union, Japan—could a nationalist and anti-imperialist policy such as Cárdenas's have been pursued without risk of becoming an instrument of this or that great power. The polarization of the world into two blocs, a fateful consequence of the Second World War, automatically eliminated the possibility of independent revolutionary movements for a long time to come.

We may turn back to the state of affairs today and attempt to decipher it. In the thirty years separating us from Cárdenism we have witnessed the gradual division of Mexico into two countries: a relatively developed one and a miserable one that is standing still. We suffer from two types of inequality: a horizontal one between one region and another (the poverty in Oaxaca, for example as compared to the average income in Sonora or Sinaloa), and a vertical one between the various classes within any one region. The undeniable economic development in this half of Mexico which is modern or on the way to modernization has created groups and classes (a middle class and a new proletariat) that have no place in the existing political structures and not even a modest share in the fabulous economic gains of recent years. Hence there is a contradiction between the social reality of these groups and the economic and political monopolies represented by the bourgeoisie and the PRI. This contradiction was the cause of the events of 1968 and the secret of the popularity of the student movement. This contradiction, in turn, is bound up with another one: the disparity between the Mexico that is developing and the Mexico that is stagnant. These two concomitant contradictions are the basic reasons for the present crisis. We cannot hope to understand the meaning of this crisis unless we are willing to concede that it is the consequence, on the one hand, of the growth of this first Mexico, and the expression, on the other hand, of the contradiction between this growth and the paralysis of this second Mexico. These two contradictions are undermining the economic and political structures on which the system of hierarchies and privileges of contemporary Mexico is based.

It is the second Mexico that has paid for the industrialization and the relative progress of the first. This second Mexico is once again beginning to be restless and rebellious. Since it has no political channels through which to express itself (it has not only been impoverished but also condemned to silence), it expresses itself by *signs* that we must interpret—from the passive gesture of emigrating to the cities to active gestures of outright violence such as kidnappings and other acts of terrorism. Terrorism, however, is not a language but a cry; what I mean to say is that it is not a solution but a weapon wielded by desperate men. The solution is political organization, something that the second Mexico can accomplish only in close alliance with dissident forces within the first Mexico. The first Mexico, in turn, must begin by taking a crucial initial step: "thawing out" popular organizations, that is to say, doing away with bureaucratic usurpations and corrupt leadership within labor organizations and other associations. To sum up: although the causes of the crisis are not identical with those that brought about the crisis that preceded Cárdenism, the method and the instrument to resolve it are similar: a popular coalition.

The very formula of a popular coalition is an implicit recognition of something that both the right and the PRI and the old left and splinter groups have stubbornly closed their eyes to: the plural nature of contemporary Mexico. There is a fundamental opposition between the real, diverse, multiple Mexico and economic, political, and ideological monolithisms. Plurality is the enemy of political monopolies (the PRI), economic monopolies (the bourgeoisie and imperialism), and ideological monopolies (sectarianisms). At the same time Mexican pluralism, the true reality of our country, is consonant with the *"détente"* of international blocs, an effort that as yet is only a timid one, but nevertheless one that promises to be halted by nothing and no one. The Russian-American hegemony is now a thing of the past. Alliances are being dissolved and new ones formed: Nixon has visited Peking, Moscow is seeking Tokyo's friendship, Western Europe will soon create an international policy of its own to implement its new power. All this means that countries such as Mexico will have a greater and greater scope for maneuver on the international scene. In this respect, too, Cárdenas's example still has much to teach us today: he managed to negotiate with both Greeks and Trojans without ever compromising our national independence.

Is a popular coalition viable? You have pointed out something of capital importance in this regard: since the days of Obregón, Mexican governments have been confronted with the two-fold need to *control* the masses (the reason behind the PRI and its bureaucratic tentacles in workers' and peasants' organizations) and at the same time to *gain their support* (the reason behind today's *"apertura democrática"*). This contradiction, which has been consistently ignored in many pseudo-Marxist analyses, is one of the conditions that make a rebirth of popular forces possible. Since this is a crucial point, I must deal with it at some length here. Although you have clearly seen the paradoxical nature of the Mexican state—this in fact is one of the most brilliant discoveries of your book—your *explanation* of this phenomenon, here again, strikes me as a mere figment of your imagination. You state: "Obregonism was the model that all subsequent governments of the Mexican bourgeoisie clung to. They were never able to crush the masses or disorganize them. They were forced not only to permit the organization of the masses but also to depend on them, by controlling them . . ." You account for this curious behavior on the part of Mexican governments as follows: "If the Russian

Revolution had not triumphed in 1917, the Mexican Revolution would not have found outside support in the world enabling it to prevent the backlash it created from becoming a rout . . ." (page 338). Frankly, no matter how hard I try, I am unable to see how Russia played any significant part in the defeat of Carranza and the victory of Obregón, in the sense of a material influence, translated into concrete facts. I am quite willing to grant that Russia had a vague ideological influence, especially on groups of middle-class intellectuals.* But you believe, and would like us to believe, that the mere existence of the Soviet Union, without any concrete action on its part, "saved" the Mexican Revolution and kept it from being stamped out by the bourgeoisie and imperialism. Aside from the fact that this is asking us to take a great deal on faith, it raises an important question: why is it that these same powers, if they

---

* I do not know whether you have read the *Memoirs* of N. Roy, the former agent of the Third International in Asia. He describes his stay in Mexico during the last years of the First World War and maintains that he played an important role in the foundation (the first one: there were two) of the Mexican Communist Party. Summoned to the Soviet Union by Lenin, he traveled on a Mexican diplomatic passport issued at the personal order of Carranza himself. This little episode proves how misleading purely ideological considerations can be.

were able to operate at a distance in this utterly intangible way (this is no more and no less than the neo-Platonist doctrine of emanations), did not save other revolutions in Europe, Asia, and America?

No, the secret of the contradictions of the Mexican state, which is forced at one and the same time to depend on the masses and to control them, does not lie in emanations of world revolution but in the very nature of that state. There is one feature that distinguishes the Mexican government from all bourgeois governments: the Party. The existence of the Party as an essential constitutive organ of the post-revolutionary Mexican state is something that still awaits proper analysis. The majority of specialists in this field evade the problem; others limit themselves to a description of it and a few disjointed remarks on the subject; still others, the Marxists, mechanically parrot the statement that the PRI and the state are merely a creation of the bourgeoisie. Being a Marxist, you too claim that the Mexican state (and therefore the PRI) is bourgeois. But you are also an intelligent Marxist, and therefore you have been obliged to resort to definitions that you yourself admit are "complicated": "Cardenism was a revolutionary nationalist and anti-imperialist government at the head of the *peculiar form of capitalist State* created by the agrarian revolution of 1910–1920" (page 351). In an earlier passage (page 345), you state: "The *peculiar characteristics* of the political apparatus of the bourgeois State created by the Revolution and forced to depend on the masses . . ." (Italics mine.) If we leave the conceptual spectacles of scholastic Marxism in their case, we shall probably find a simpler explanation of the *peculiarities* of the Mexican state, an explanation that, as you will see, views them as merely a particular instance of a general phenomenon: the appearance of bureaucratic states throughout the world in the twentieth century.

The Party is a bureaucracy of specialists whose particular field is the organization and the manipulation of masses. Its influence extends horizontally over the entire country, and it reaches down vertically to the *ejidos,* the labor unions, municipal governments, and cooperatives. Throughout all its many avatars and changes of color (PNR, PRM, and PRI), its function has remained the same: it is the organ for controlling the masses, but at the same time, up until a few years ago, it was also the masses' organ of expression, though an imperfect one. The most immediate and most crucial aspect of the current crisis in Mexico is precisely the fact that the PRI, while continuing to control the masses, has entirely ceased to express their will. In any case, the fact that the Party has survived is proof that it is an essential organ of the post-revolutionary Mexican state.

On the one hand, this is a feature which *distinguishes* it from all the bourgeois states; on the other hand, it is a feature that it *shares* with the so-called "Socialist" countries of Eastern Europe and elsewhere. This feature also appears, in a less pure form, in all those countries of the Third World in which popular revolutions or movements of national liberation have triumphed—in Egypt, for instance. Since I have dealt with this subject elsewhere, I will here merely point out that the birth of political bureaucracies in the twentieth century is the result of revolutions in countries that were not sufficiently developed and lacked democratic traditions. The Party, in the special sense that that word has acquired in our century, is the result of two "failures" of the theory of historical development, one international and the other national: the absence of a proletarian revolution in the developed countries and, in the others, the absence (or the weakness) of a native bourgeoisie capable of effectively carrying out the industrialization and the modernization of their country. In countries where this phenomenon manifests itself in its purest form, as in Russia, revolution liquidates the weak bourgeoisie and the political bureaucracy takes over the direction of the state and the economy; in other cases, as in Mexico, the political bureaucracy becomes, at one and the same time, the ally and the rival of the bourgeoisie and never entirely fuses with it. In both cases the bureaucracy proclaims itself the heir and the continuer of the revolutionary movement. In *The Other Mexico*, and even before, in *The Labyrinth of Solitude,* I have pointed out that the post-revolutionary Mexican bourgeoisie is at least in part a child of the Mexican state. What I have not shown clearly is the dialectics of opposition/alliance that ties the state and the bourgeoisie to each other without in any way fusing them. This is the counterpart of the other contradictory relation that you have discovered: the fact that the state (and the Party) must alternately depend on the masses and control them.

As you are well aware, the phenomenon of a bureaucratic society was of great concern to Trotsky. We find an early formulation of the problem in *The Revolution Betrayed*. Later on, shortly before he was murdered, since the subject had provoked bitter dissension within the Fourth International, Trotsky devoted an article to it, his last theoretical text (*The Soviet Union at War,* 1939). I shall briefly summarize his point of view. Confronted with the fact that Soviet society had become hierarchical and authoritarian, Trotsky pondered the problem of its real nature, that is to say, its social makeup, the relations between classes and the means of production and the characteristic features of the class that was clearly dominating the country economically and politically. After discarding the hypothesis that this was state capitalism, he arrived at the conclusion that it was a proletarian state that had degenerated, "a contradictory society halfway between capitalism and Socialism." A proletariat state because the workers had come into power without having entirely completed the transition to Socialism; a degenerate state because "even though the means of production belong to the State, the State, in a manner of speaking, belongs to the bureaucracy." The degeneration, the social disease that the state and society were suffering from, was bureaucracy and its visible incarnation, the Party Secretary, Stalin. But the disease was not a constitutional one: Trotsky steadfastly refused to consider the bureaucracy a class, since its domination was not founded on the ownership of the means of production. The state bureaucrats were a caste that had usurped power, and thus their rule was not a genuine historical alternative. Situated at this halfway point between capitalism and Socialism, the Soviet Union would resolve the contradiction that was tearing it apart either by bringing about the victory of Socialism (by liquidating the Stalinist bureaucracy that had usurped power) or by restoring capitalism. But neither of these two developments has in fact occurred.

In the last days of his life, in the course of his polemical skirmishing with certain members of the United States section of the Fourth International, Trotsky's point of view changed in certain respects, and he recognized a third possibility (though he regarded it as a very remote one): "bureaucratic collectivism." Trotsky borrowed this expression from Bruno R.,* an Italian revolutionary who was the author of a little-known but widely plagiarized book: *La bureaucratisation du monde (The Bureaucratization of the World, 1939)*. Throughout his article Trotsky more or less repeated this author's arguments in support of the contention that the bureaucracy

---

* Early in 1946, when I was working in the Mexican Embassy in Paris, I came across a manuscript in a cabinet where "secret papers" were filed: a typewritten copy of this book by Bruno Rizzi (his full name), along with a cover letter to the Minister of Mexico in France at the time, who, if I remember correctly, was Luis I. Rodríguez, Cárdenas's former secretary. In his letter, Bruno Rizzi asked the Mexican diplomat, "the representative of Cárdenas's popular democratic government," to see that a copy of his still unpublished manuscript reached Trotsky. He insisted that it was of vital importance that the Russian revolutionary read his work, and added that he was relying on diplomatic channels because he knew of no other safe way to get a copy to him: he was certain that he was being followed by police from all over the world and foresaw that Europe would soon be engulfed in a wave of totalitarianism. I presume that Rodríguez complied with Rizzi's request.

was not a class but a caste. Trotsky also criticized Bruno R., however, for ignoring all the differences separating the Soviet Union from Germany and Italy, despite all the apparent similarities between the three regimes: in Russia the state owned the means of production, whereas in the latter two countries capitalist ownership had remained intact. Nonetheless, at the end of his article he stated that if the bureaucratic regime should prove to be a new form of social oppression and not simply a temporary reactionary excrescence within the proletariat state, and if, at the same time, "the international proletariat should prove truly incapable of fulfilling the function assigned it by the development of historical forces, one would be obliged to frankly recognize that the Socialist program, based on overcoming the internal contradictions of capitalist society, has in the end proven to be a utopia." And he added, with his usual forthrightness and generosity: "In such a case, it would be necessary to formulate a new minimal program to defend the slaves of totalitarian bureaucratic society." If Trotsky were still alive today, I do not know what he would call the Soviet Union and the countries over which it holds sway, but I for my part must frankly confess that calling them "proletariat States," as you do, strikes me as a pious self-delusion.

The survival of Soviet bureaucracy and its spread to many other countries is proof that it is not a transitory illness of the state born of revolution. But if it is not a caste, what is it? Many writers—Djilas being the most recent among them —have maintained that the bureaucrats must be regarded, willy-nilly, as a class, the "new class." It is hard to decide who is right. On the one hand, the "Socialist" bureaucracy does not own the means of production and therefore cannot perpetuate itself by handing down its possessions to its children, as other classes have done in previous periods of history. On the other hand, however, since it totally dominates the state, it in effect owns the means of production and has no need of title deeds. It perpetuates itself not through inheritance but through education and other means that give its sons and daughters a privileged place within the little closed circle of the dominant group. The privileged historical status of the bureaucracy is "illegitimate," but doesn't the same thing happen in capitalist societies? The bourgeoisie governs in the name of the people and the bureaucracy in the name of the proletariat. And finally, there is one thing that cannot be gainsaid: whether a caste or a class, the bureaucrats are possessed of a remarkable social cohesion that distinguishes and separates them from other groups and strata within the society . . . It is tempting to equate the "Socialist" bureaucracies with the technocracies of the West as described by J. K. Galbraith and other economists. The differences, however, are no less significant than the similarities. Among these differences: Soviet bureaucracy was the result of a revolution in an insufficiently developed country surrounded by enemies, whereas technocracies are an outcome of advanced capitalism. Another difference: the technocrats control the large corporations and go on from there to take over the capitalist state—they start out in the field of economics and technology and then turn to politics; the bureaucrats, on the other hand, control the state and go on from there to dominate economic life—they go from politics to technology and economics. In the end, however, these two divergent movements have similar results: both lead to the technico-bureaucratic state in which international hegemony, and therefore military considerations, come first.

What about the political bureaucracy in Mexico? It is clearly not a class in the traditional sense of the word. Nor can it properly be described as a caste. [This is also true of the "Socialist" bureaucracies: they are not really *castes*. If we wish to preserve the precise meaning of such a term, it should be applied only to the castes (*jeti*) of India.] Although the Mexican political bureaucracy is not a class, it is indeed a relatively independent social entity displaying unique and distinctive features. From the social point of view, what distinguishes this group is not its ownership of the means of production or the fact that it is made up of workers and employees, but rather the fact that it controls popular organizations on every level, from the lowest to the highest. It is a society within a society. Although it lacks a coherent ideology and a "world-view"—that great invisible cement of churches and in our day of "Socialist" bureaucracies—its social cohesion is such that it can withstand both changes of direction and moral crises. The Party has changed course ideologically at least three times (PNR, PRM, and PRI) without serious schisms and without its discipline being undermined. Though the intellectual fabric of the Party may be wispy and subject to constant change, its social fabric is extremely durable and unchanging. The social background of the groups going to make up the Party has not varied since it was first founded forty years ago: these groups come from the petty bourgeoisie, and to a lesser extent from the elite of workers and peasants. Though it is closely allied today with the bourgeoisie, the Party is not an association of bourgeois or of property-owners. Its leaders eventually become both, but once they do, they cease to be active in politics and devote their time to their "business interests." A hierarchical but at the same time an open society, a society that puts those who have little or nothing on the road to privilege and power, partly a religious order and partly an employment agency, a brotherhood and a mutual benefit society, the Party gives its members a sense of social identity. This is precious, for it is something that the modern world denies people: the security of knowing that they are part of a community, which in turn gives them a feeling of self-assurance as individuals. The alienation, in the strict sense of that much-abused word, of which the Party is an instrument is a twofold one: its members identify with something *other* than themselves, but so does the Party itself. What I mean to say is this: it does not conceive of itself as a *party* among other parties, a part of Mexico, but rather as a totality—it is the entire nation with its past, its present, and its future. The Party is the Revolution and the Past and the Future, it is Juárez and Doña Josefa Ortiz de Domínguez, Madero and Montezuma, the Pyramids of Teotihuacán and the Monument to the Mother. All times and spaces: all contradictions are dissolved within its bosom. It is the Nation as a whole: outside of the Party Mexicans have no political reality and no historical reality.

Despite this claim to be the Nation itself, the Party lives in precarious balance between the bourgeoisie and the masses: its interests lie with the former and its possibility of survival with the latter. Hence it does not totally identify itself with either. This contradictory situation is not unique in history. We might even say that this has been the fate of all the great political bureaucracies of the past. For more than two thousand years the Chinese Mandarins lived in a state of perpetual rivalry and compromise with other social powers and forces. Like the PRI, they were obliged to seek the support of the masses in order to withstand their rivals, come to terms with them, or destroy them: the old feudal aristocracy first of all, then later the "eunuch party," and at all times the army. The Sinologist Etienne Balazs has written a book on the subject that indirectly sheds a great deal of light on the history of our twentieth century [*La bureaucratie céleste* (*Bureaucracy in the Heavenly Kingdom*), 1969]. It is worth digressing for a moment and taking a closer look at the Mandarin regime in ancient China. Three conclusions can be drawn, it seems to me, from Balazs's book, and all three, as will be seen, are pertinent to the present situation in Mexico and other parts of the world.

The first conclusion has to do with the stages of historical evolution. The usual claim is that there is an inexorable and necessary process leading mankind from a society based on slavery to feudalism, and then successively to capitalism, socialism, and so on. To a certain degree, the so-called Chu period can be regarded as the equivalent of feudalism in the West, but the crisis marking the last days of feudal society in China did not come to an end because of the triumph of capitalism but rather because of the emergence of the Mandarin bureaucracy. Max Weber and the American Sinologist Joseph R. Levenson had arrived at similar conclusions in their analyses of Chinese society. Hence the process is not inevitable and necessary (history is not entirely predictable), and we cannot justifiably speak of a single process of development governing all societies: world history is proof, on the contrary, of a plurality of paths and directions. The theory of a single process of development is an ethnocentric theory whereby the historical model of the West is indiscriminately applied to all societies. The second conclusion has to do with the ambiguous nature of the relations between the Mandarins and other classes and social forces and with the remarkable permanence of this system of pacts, alliances, and compromises. From the proclamation of the Chin dynasty in 246 B.C. to the proclamation of the Republic in 1912, the Mandarins remained in power, but their power was never absolute, and their regime was based on a continual unstable compromise with other groups and classes. To a certain extent this proves Trotsky's contention: bureaucracy is an exceptional regime that never resolves the basic contradictions of a given society. China under the Mandarins was a society halfway between feudalism and capitalism. But a regime that endures for more than two thousand years cannot be labeled a *transitory* one, however reluctant we may be to grant that fact. And finally, thanks to their relative independence from the Imperial Throne, Chinese bureaucrats were able to create the institution of censorship (of the Emperor), and Mandarin men of letters instituted the noble tradition of criticism of those in power. In places where bureaucracy has no rivals, as in the "Socialist" countries, it suppresses criticism. The (relative) freedom of criticism that we enjoy in Mexico stems from the same factors that enabled the Mandarins to institute censorship of the Emperor: by that I mean to say that it is as much a consequence of the social and political pluralism of our country as of the paradoxical situation confronting the group that holds the reins of government.

It is important to stress the relative independence of the Mexican State and its political organ, the Party, because otherwise we may fail to appreciate the real nature of the present dichotomy. If it is true that the state is subject to the contradiction that obliges it both to seek the support of the masses and to control them, we must face up to the logical conclusion that follows from this state of affairs: the state seeks the support of the masses in order to *stand up to* or *oppose* the bourgeoisie and imperialism; and at the same time, the state controls the masses in order to *co-exist* or *reach some sort of agreement* with these latter. This is the dilemma of the state and the Party, but *it is not the dilemma* of the bourgeoisie. The choice confronting the bourgeoisie is different: governing with the state and the PRI or without them. But if they are to govern without them, whom else can they rely on? The army or para-military groups and forces such as The Falcons. Hence the two real alternatives are democratic social reform or reactionary violence. The left quite heedlessly engages in purely verbal acts of violence, and with the recent kidnappings, in symbolic acts of violence. But the real danger of subversion lies in the other direction: the bourgeoisie may be tempted to break off its alliance with the PRI and resort to force. Have you read *Tiempo mexicano* (*Mexican Time*), Carlos Fuentes's recent book? In these pages political journalism takes on a literary range—at once epic, satirical, lyrical, passionate—that it has not had for many years, either in our language or in others. (Norman Mailer, writing in English, might be another example—but who is there in France?) One of the most impressive texts in this book is "La muerte de Rubén Jaramillo" ("The Death of Rubén Jaramillo").* This is the other alternative in Mexico, and we must fight against

---

* Rubén Jaramillo: a peasant leader assassinated in 1962.

it. I repeat: we will have either an independent popular coalition or authoritarian violence.

I have mentioned the economic advances of the last few decades a number of times. I shall now return to the subject, but this time I would like to deal with it from another point of view: that of the search for different models of development. For a number of years now Mexicans (I am thinking here of those who belong to the more or less highly developed portion of the country) have had personal experience of what an industrial society entails. In the beginning, they greeted this society with enthusiasm; today many Mexicans look upon it with great misgiving, and others with horror. The experience has been negative. I shall not repeat what you are already quite aware of: the inconveniences, the anxieties, the penalties, the dangers, the ignominy, the crimes, the psychic contamination, the air pollution . . . People who live in Mexico City are beginning to have some idea of what it is like to live in New York, Moscow, or Tokyo. As a result, not only capitalist development but also the very notion of development has come under fire. This sort of criticism is not found among Marxists, who believe in progress and technology; it does appear, on the other hand, in so-called "utopian Socialism." The harmonious society is not a progress-oriented society, although Fourier was eager to make scientific progress the basis of his Harmony. No one, however, seriously advocates that we give up the benefits of science. And even if we wanted to, we could not get along without technology: we are doomed to live with it and by it. But we are not doomed to be its slaves. The tradition of "utopian Socialism" takes on new significance in our day and age because it views man not only as the producer and the worker but as a creature with desires and dreams: passion is one of the central axes of any society because it is a force of attraction and repulsion. Using this conception of the passionate man as a point of departure, we can conceive of societies governed by a type of rationality that is different from the technological rationality of the twentieth century. In the East as in the West, the criticism of society that is taking shape is leading to a search for viable models of development different from those predominate today.

I would like to point out that when I speak of *viable* models, I mean models that are not imaginary even though they may not be realizable in the immediate future. Nor are they ideal geometries outside of space and time. In many instances, these models already exist in social practice, if only in a rudimentary form. I will give an example of what I have in mind. On page 358 of *La revolución interrumpida,* you write: "The continued existence of the *ejido* is not due to the fact that it has been an economic success . . . It is

not an economic but a social question. It is not a
matter of economics, but a matter, rather, of the
peasant's determination not to regress to a system
of private ownership, and the support that this
determination has earned within the world revolutionary movement . . ." You have again discovered the key, but immediately thereafter your
progressivist and historicist beliefs have impelled
you to bury your original insight beneath more or
less fanciful remarks concerning historical development. (You will note that what you regard as
real, as obeying a rational principle because it is
subject to supposed laws of history, in every case
strikes me as *ideal,* or rather, as an ideological
fantasy.) The survival of the *ejido* is explainable
not in terms of the influence of the world revolutionary movement, but on historical, cultural, and
anthropological grounds: the *ejido* system of ownership is closely linked to the traditional social
organization and the equally traditional ethical
system governing social and family relations
among Mexican peasants. But this is not my principal point. You are quite right when you state
that it is not an economic but a social question.
This is true: the rationale behind the *ejido* is different from the modern economic rationale based
on profit and productivity. The *ejido* is not a perfect model from the economic point of view: it
is, rather, a possible model of a harmonious so-

ciety. The *ejido* is inferior to the capitalist system of agriculture if we use the production of more bushels of rice or alfalfa as the measuring rod; it is not inferior if what matters to us is the creation of human values and the establishment of less oppressive, more just, and freer relations between human beings. I am not saying that we must toss the concept of profit and other economic notions out the window; I would merely like to point out that these concepts are not, and should not be, the only ones to be taken into consideration. Classical economists claimed that the free enterprise system had an *implicit* rationale, and enslaved men in the name of this rationale; the planned economies of the "Socialist" countries are said to be based on an *explicit* rationale, and have enslaved millions in its name. But in all of this, where does reason enter the picture? It is the *ejido* and analogous social forms that have reason on their side.

All of the above is meant to show you where I agree and where I disagree with you. Among the points of disagreement, I would say that the principal one is my refusal to go along with the central idea underlying your book: the vision of history as a rational discourse whose subject is world revolution and whose protagonist is the international proletariat. No, I do not believe that history unfolds in an absolutely orderly way, be it the linear order of evolutionism (a biological theory that is mechanically applied to history) or that of dialectics. There are no historical or social laws in the same sense that there are physical and biological laws. I think it quite possible that society may be governed by more or less constant tendencies, by recurrences and variations that, with certain reservations, might be called social laws. These laws, however, have yet to be discovered. And if they ever are discovered, will they be applicable to history? They may well be, although there is another difficulty involved that must not be underestimated: the sphere of anthropology and sociology is that of the synchronic, whereas the realm of history is that of the diachronic—to use two very fashionable scholarly terms. History is diachronic: variation, change. It is the world of the unpredictable and the unique, the region in which the historic day *par excellence* is "the one we least expect." Hence it gives rise to the feeling (or perhaps the delusion) that it is the realm of freedom: history presents itself to us as the possibility of choice. You chose Socialism—and that is why you are in prison. This fact leads me to make a choice too: to condemn the society that has put you behind prison bars. Thus, at certain moments at least, our philosophical and political differences dissolve and can be reconciled in a single statement: it is necessary to fight against a society that jails dissidents.

It is time to bring this letter to a close. I

hope that when I return to Mexico, we may continue this conversation, out in the fresh open air.
If that is not possible, I will come visit you in
your cell in Lecumberri—that prison that Jack
Womack says is turning into our Institute of Political Sciences.

Cordially,

OCTAVIO PAZ
—Translated by HELEN R. LANE